ECONOMIC ISSUES, PROBLEMS AND PERSPECTIVES

ECONOMICS OF ENVIRONMENTAL POLICY IN OLIGOPOLISTIC MARKETS

ECONOMIC ISSUES, PROBLEMS AND PERSPECTIVES

Additional books in this series can be found on Nova's website under the Series tab.

Additional e-books in this series can be found on Nova's website under the e-books tab.

ECONOMIC ISSUES, PROBLEMS AND PERSPECTIVES

ECONOMICS OF ENVIRONMENTAL POLICY IN OLIGOPOLISTIC MARKETS

MAHELET G. FIKRU
AND
MATT INSALL
EDITORS

nova publishers
New York

NOTICE TO THE READER

Library of Congress Cataloging-in-Publication Data

ISBN: 978-1-63463-165-5

Published by Nova Science Publishers, Inc. † New York

CONTENTS

PREFACE

With the rising public and political concern about greener production, there is unrelenting pressure on individual companies to abate pollution and adopt cleaner technologies. Governments adopt several types of environmental policies and regulations that are aimed at protecting the environment and encouraging efficient use of natural resources. Instruments such as carbon tax, emission quota and abatement subsidy are being proposed and implemented in several countries. Such policies affect firms' strategic decision-making such as creating joint ventures, product differentiation, R&D, expansion and outsourcing. This book examines the relationship between firms' strategic decision making, environmental policies and resulting effect on the society. Each chapter builds a theoretical model in which the market structure is imperfect competition.

Chapter 1 considers a horizontally differentiated Cournot model to examine (i) the role of firms' abatement efforts on the characterization of optimal emission tax and (ii) the adjustment of optimal policy as products become differentiated. The analysis indicates that in the presence of abatement efforts the government may afford a tax reduction to address output distortion as products become more differentiated. Additionally, the analysis suggests that policies which may encourage firms to differentiate themselves as environmentally conscious may aid in the reduction of industry emissions, and at the same time allow a reduction in emission tax to address output distortion present in imperfectly competitive markets.

Chapter 2 considers the joint effect of profit and emission taxation in a model of imperfect competition with environmental externalities. The chapter shows that, when both profit taxation and emission taxation are used, the former is no longer neutral. The two fiscal tools are substitutes, and for any profit taxation rate there exists a unique optimal environmental tax rate that entails the first best outcome as equilibrium. The analysis therefore suggests that policy makers in charge of different taxation policies should coordinate in order to optimally design the tax menu for firms. This chapter finds that profit taxation has no consequence on firms' green R&D efforts for the attainment of abatement technologies. In this regard, the chapter also shows that independent R&D projects accompanied by information sharing (i.e., technological spillovers) outperform a joint venture when a green innovation is at stake.

Chapter 3 examines the effect of pollution quota and pollution tax on social welfare of two different countries. Results indicate that pollution policies restrict trade, reduce producer surplus, consumer surplus and pollution. Optimal quota will be higher as pollution and efficiency of local firms is lower; optimal tax rate will be higher as tax revenue and the harming pollution are higher. When tax revenue and pollution are low, the government would be willing to offer a subsidy in order to encourage consumer and producer surplus. The chapter emphasizes the importance of establishing strategic rational environmental policies in order to maximize the competitiveness of firms, expected benefits for consumers and to minimize the impact of pollution.

Chapter 4 discusses inter-industry pollution and corresponding environmental protection policies with the consideration of a budget constraint. The chapter shows that in the short run with no budget constraint, the output quantity based subsidy distorts the price mechanism because non-polluters will expand production as much as possible to claim the subsidy, so that their profit is maximized. Such a result raises concerns for heavier fiscal burden and the unfairness of a society. When a budget constraint is considered to tackle the concerns, the government will pay the subsidy with caution and impose higher tax on polluting firms. Thus the environmental protection is strengthened and the short-run distortion rectified in the case with no budget constraint.

Chapter 5 presents a model of acquisition decisions when environmental policy such as a carbon tax is present. The result of this chapter suggests that carbon tax can affect acquisition decisions where the exact relationship between the tax and acquisition (dis)incentives depends on the pollution intensity of the acquisition partners. Furthermore the results of this chapter suggest that there may be perverse incentive situations, namely cases in which dirtier firms profitably acquire cleaner firms without making use of their cleaner technology.

In: Economics of Environmental Policy ... ISBN: 978-1-63463-165-5
Editors: M. G. Fikru and M. Insall

Chapter 1

HORIZONTAL PRODUCT DIFFERENTIATION, POLLUTION ABATEMENT AND EMISSION TAXES UNDER COURNOT OLIGOPOLY

Luis Gautier*
Department of Social Sciences, University of Texas - Tyler,
Tyler, Texas, US

Abstract

There is an increasing number of firms across a variety of industries, which are taking steps to differentiate themselves as environmentally conscious firms, both to achieve gains from product differentiation and to reduce production and pollution abatement costs. In light of this trend in many industries, this chapter considers a horizontally differentiated Cournot model to examine (i) the role of pollution abatement efforts by firms on the characterization of the optimal emission tax and (ii) the adjustment of optimal policy as products become differentiated. The analysis indicates that in the presence of abatement efforts by firms the government may afford a tax reduction to address the output distortion as products become more differentiated. Additionally, the analysis suggests that policies which may encourage firms to differentiate themselves as environmentally conscious firms may aid in the reduction of industry emissions, and at the same time allow a reduction in the emission tax to address the output distortion present in imperfectly competitive markets.

*E-mail address: lgautier@uttyler.edu

JEL Classification: H23, L13, Q58

Keywords: Horizontal product differentiation, Cournot, Emission taxes, Environmental policy

1. Introduction

There is an increasing number of firms across a variety of industries, which are taking steps to differentiate themselves as environmentally conscious firms, both to achieve gains from product differentiation and to reduce production and pollution abatement costs (e.g., Eriksson, 2004; Conrad, 2005; Lyon and Maxwell, 2008; Portney, 2008; Lambertini, 2013). In many cases these firms operate in imperfectly competitive markets characterized by horizontal product differentiation and, at the same time, face carbon pricing policies such as emission taxes (e.g., Thollander and Ottosson, 2008; USDOC, 2010). As a result of the continued efforts by some of these firms to (i) differentiate themselves as environmentally conscious and (ii) engage in pollution abatement activities, traditional market-based environmental policies may need to account for these two aspects and adapt accordingly. This chapter considers a horizontally differentiated Cournot model, in the spirit of Fujiwara (2009), to examine the role of pollution abatement efforts by firms on the characterization of the optimal emission tax and the adjustment of optimal policy as products become differentiated. The analysis indicates that with sufficient abatement efforts by firms the government may lower the optimal emission tax in order to address the output distortion as products become more differentiated.

The literature of environmental policy under Cournot oligopolistic conditions is vast. In the context of a closed economy, one strand examines the characterization of optimal taxation assuming homogeneous goods but putting aside abatement efforts (e.g., Levine, 1985; Simpson, 1995; Lee, 1999), and including abatement efforts but ruling out the possibility of differentiated products (e.g., Ebert, 1992; Katsoulacos and Xepapadeas, 1995). A second strand incorporates horizontal product differentiation but assumes away abatement efforts by firms (e.g., Eriksson, 2004; Fujiwara, 2009; Espínola-Arrendondo and Zhau, 2012). The contribution of the present chapter is at the intersection of these two strands.

In a formal sense the present chapter is closest to Fujiwara (2009) where abatement efforts are assumed away and the conditions under which the optimal tax may fall/rise with more differentiated markets are derived. The author shows that in the case of exogenous number of firms the optimal tax may be positive or negative (subsidization), and that it may rise or fall as products become more differentiated depending on whether the government puts more weight on damages from pollution vis-à-vis the output distortion. Crucially, the present work differs from Fujiwara's in that abatement efforts are considered through two channels, namely, the direct reduction in marginal abatement costs (e.g., via cost-reducing environmental research and development or $R\&D$) and the ability of firms to differentiate themselves as environmentally conscious firms. These two important aspects, which are increasingly present in a number of industries, alter the characterization of optimal policy and the extent to which it falls or rises as products become more differentiated. It is noteworthy that these channels are assumed to be exogenous in the model since the strategic choice of abatement (e.g., cost-reducing environmental $R\&D$) has been analyzed elsewhere (e.g., Carlsson, 2000; Montero, 2002a, 2002b; Poyago-Theotoky, 2003; Ulph and Ulph, 1996, 2007; Yakita and Yamauchi, 2011).

Ebert (1992) points out in a rather general setting that, in the presence of abatement technologies and assuming away product differentiation, the optimal tax may be higher because of the abatement incentives provided by the tax; this result is important because it indicates the important role of abatement efforts in the characterization of policy. The present work builds from this important result by considering a more specific setting which allows to derive, among others, specific conditions under which the optimal policy is taxation and examine the role of product differentiation on abatement and, therefore, optimal policy, two aspects which have received little attention in the literature. Simpson (1995) and Levine (1985), among others, examine the effects of emission taxes on industry emissions assuming away abatement efforts and product differentiation, two important aspects in a number of industries. There is also a small literature which incorporates horizontal product differentiation, but differs from the present setting in that the analysis is undertaken in an international context (e.g, Lahiri and Symeonidis, 2007; Gautier, 2013) or in the presence of policies other than emission taxes (e.g., abatement subsidies) and assuming the strategic choice of $R\&D$ (e.g., Poyago-Theotoky, 2003). The present work assumes away the strategic interaction of the choice of $R\&D$ and the role of the abatement subsidy, and the focus is on how exogenous changes in the degree of product differentiation (e.g., firms differentiate themselves as environmentally conscious firms) may alter abatement efforts, the characterization of policy and consequently industry emissions.

A second contribution of this chapter is that it presents a systematic analysis of how changes in the degree of product differentiation affect industry emissions via adjustments in the optimal tax as well as the direct effect (for given tax). To see this consider the case where firms differentiate their products. As a result, output in this market rises, thereby raising emissions, if abatement efforts are assumed away. If in order to tackle higher emissions the government raises the tax, then industry emission may fall and, as a result, the change in industry emissions, arising from an exogenous change in the degree of product differentiation may not be clear-cut. Additionally, the inclusion of abatement efforts into the model changes the characterization of policy and consequently the extent to which the government adjusts the tax with more differentiated products.

The analysis indicates that abatement efforts play an important role in the characterization of the optimal tax, particularly in the case where changes in the degree of horizontal product differentiation works via changes in the pollution intensity coefficient i.e., environmentally conscious firms. It is shown that policy induced abatement efforts may result in taxation by the government even in the case where sufficient weight is put on addressing the output distortion. Additionally, the analysis indicates that in the presence of abatement efforts the government can afford a tax reduction as products become more differentiated even when damages to the environment is a concern to the government. As a result, industry emissions are likely to increase even when abatement efforts by firms are sufficiently large. One policy implication from the analysis is that additional policies might be needed if a reduction in industry emissions is to be achieved as products become more differentiated.

The chapter is structured as follows. The next section spells out the model and section 3 presents some of the comparative static results. Section 4 characterizes the optimal emission tax and examines its adjustment as products become more differentiated. Section 5 analyzes the effect of policy adjustment on industry emissions. The last section concludes.

2. The Model

Consider an industry with a fixed number of firms $n > 1$ operating under Cournot oligopolistic conditions in the presence of horizontal product differentiation. Each firm i $(i = 1, 2, \dots, n)$ engages in the production of an imperfect substitute or variety i, which is sold in the domestic market; each firm also generates pollution and consequently additional costs to society, but also engages in pollution abatement activities. We shall follow Fujiwara (2009) in the structure of the demand function (see also Cellini et al., 2004); in particular, inverse demand faced by each firm i comes from preferences such that $p^i = \alpha - (\beta - \gamma)q^i - \gamma \sum q^i$, satisfying $\beta > \gamma > 0$, $\alpha > 0$ $\forall i$, where γ represents the degree of product differentiation. As it is standard in the literature, $\gamma \simeq 0$ captures the case where products become very differentiated, and $\gamma \simeq \beta$ the case of homogeneous goods. q_i denotes output of variety i produced by firm i. The government and firms play a two-stage game where the government sets policy optimally (i.e., per-unit emission tax) through social welfare maximization, and firms then take policy as given and maximize profits by simultaneously choosing the level of output and emissions. Throughout we shall analyze the symmetric equilibrium, assume interior solutions and that firms behave in a Cournot-Nash fashion.

To capture pollution abatement efforts by firms, we shall assume the end-of-pipe cost function is defined as $C^i = \tilde{c}^i q^i + z^i(\delta^i(\gamma)q^i - e^i)^2/2$ where $\tilde{c} > 0$, $z \geq 1$, $\delta' > 0$, $\delta'' = 0$. The first term captures production costs and the second abatement costs, where units of pollution abated are given by $a^i = \delta^i q^i - e^i$. Several remarks about the cost function are in order. First, it satisfies the usual concavity assumptions; and second it captures abatement efforts through two different channels.[1] The first channel consists of the pollution intensity coefficient, δ, which is assumed to depend positively and linearly on the degree of product differentiation, γ. This means that firms may seek to differentiate themselves by being environmentally conscious via a lower pollution intensity coefficient i.e., $\delta = \delta(\gamma)$ where $\delta'(\gamma) > 0$ (we shall touch on the effects of this on firm behavior later on). Important examples include companies like Patagonia and Whole Foods, which differentiate themselves as environmentally sustainable companies, and Wal-Mart and Costco have made the commitment to lower energy consumption through solar lighting and heating (Portney, 2008: 263). Additionally, companies may also differentiate themselves to avoid negative public opinion (Portney, 2008; Lyon and Maxwell, 2008). The second channel is via the direct reduction in pollution abatement costs; in particular, a large (small) value of z denotes less (more) abatement efforts by each firm since a large (small) value of z translates into an increase (reduction) in pollution abatement costs. It is noteworthy that neither of these channels intends to capture the strategic decisions of firms to increase/decrease abatement efforts

[1] See Requate (2006) for the properties of the cost function and Lahiri and Symeonidis (2007) for examples of end-of-pipe cost functions.

and so they are exogenous in the model. The reason for this assumption via a specific cost function is threefold. First, the strategic decision of environmental R&D and differentiated products have been examined elsewhere (e.g., Carlsson, 2000; Montero, 2000a, 2000b; Conrad, 2005; Ulph and Ulph, 2007). Second, specific functional forms allows to track the potential role of abatement efforts in the presence of product differentiation, one of the main objectives of this chapter, and analyze the effects of different pollution abatement efforts (channels) by firms and their impact on optimal policy. By modeling these two channels we are able to compare some results with the existing literature and at the same time derive some new results.

Each firm i maximizes profits by choosing e^i and q^i in a Cournot-Nash fashion:

$$\max_{q^i e^i} \pi^i = p^i q^i - C^i(q^i, e^i) - \tau e^i - f^i \tag{1}$$

where f^i denotes fixed costs and τ the emission tax set by the government. This yields two first-order conditions, which under symmetry are given by

$$p - \beta q - \tilde{c} - \delta z(\delta q - e) = 0 \tag{2}$$

$$z(\delta q - e) - \tau = 0 \tag{3}$$

where $p = \alpha - q(\beta + \gamma(n-1))$. These implicitly determine the equilibrium level of output, q, emissions, e, and therefore abatement, a, and have the usual interpretation. In particular, the tax is equal to marginal abatement costs, and marginal revenue equals marginal production costs. Since the number of firms is fixed, total output, $Q = nq$, total emissions, $E = ne$, and total abatement, $A = na$, are also implicitly determined. Notice that in (3) a small ratio $1/z$ (large z) simply says that, for given tax, the firm engages in less direct abatement efforts since a large z increases abatement costs thereby lowering equilibrium abatement; conversely, a large ratio $1/z$, captures the idea that the firm engages in more abatement efforts via lower abatement costs.[2] For completeness, we include the expression for the Cournot-Nash equilibrium level of output, q, which will aid in the analysis presented in subsequent sections. In particular, (2) and (3) yield $q = (\alpha - \tilde{c} - \delta\tau)/D$ where $D = 2\beta + \gamma(n-1) > 0$.

[2]Formally, for $z \geq 1$ the ratio $1/z \in (0, 1]$.

3. Comparative Statics

The comparative statics effects are obtained via differentiation of (2) and (3). In particular, the effects of the tax and degree of product differentiation (for given tax) on output and emissions are given by

$$Ddq = -\delta d\tau - \left[q(n-1) + \tau\delta'\right] d\gamma \tag{4}$$

$$Dde = -\left[\delta^2 + D/z\right] d\tau + \left[Dq\delta' - \delta\delta'\tau - \delta q(n-1)\right] d\gamma \tag{5}$$

where $D = 2\beta + \gamma(n-1) > 0$. There are two main effects at play. First, an increase in the tax raises production costs via higher tax payments and, as a result, output and emissions fall; the larger (smaller) the pollution intensity coefficient the more (less) firms will have to pay in taxes. Second, the tax raises the incentives for pollution abatement and, as a result, emissions fall via the term $1/z$. Notice that this effect becomes smaller (larger) as firms engage in less (more) direct abatement i.e., the ratio $1/z$ becomes smaller (larger).

As products become more differentiated (i.e., decrease in γ), output rises because, on the one hand, firms are differentiated and on the other a smaller δ' (i.e., as firms differentiate themselves and become more environmentally conscious) reduces production costs. In terms of emissions there are two opposing effects at play here. On the one hand, with more differentiated products output and therefore emissions rise; and on the other, the pollution intensity coefficient falls as firms seek to become more environmentally conscious. This has two effects in turn. A smaller pollution intensity coefficient results in (i) lower costs in the form of less tax payments and, as a result, higher output and therefore emissions; and (ii) lower marginal abatement costs (i.e., a downward shift in the marginal abatement cost function) and thus lower emissions. If firms are pollution-moderate and sufficiently environmentally conscious (i.e., δ small and δ' large), then emissions may fall via more abatement as a result of differentiated products; formally (subscript denotes partial derivative), $e_\gamma > 0$ *if and only if* $\delta' > \delta(\alpha - \tilde{c} - \delta\tau)(n-1)/D(\alpha - \tilde{c} - 2\delta\tau)$.[3] Intuitively, a lower intensity coefficient, δ, controls the increase in emissions (which takes place with

[3] Analogously, $e_\gamma < 0 \Leftrightarrow \delta' < \delta(\alpha - \tilde{c} - \delta\tau)(n-1)/D(\alpha - \tilde{c} - 2\delta\tau)$, where it is assumed that $\alpha - \tilde{c} - 2\delta\tau > 0$. A sensitive δ with respect to γ (i.e., δ' large) captures the idea that firms are relatively more environmentally conscious, whereas a small (less sensitive) δ' captures the case where firms are less environmentally conscious. As firms differentiate themselves (this is captured via a decrease in γ) they become more environmentally conscious which results in a reduction in the pollution intensity coefficient, δ. Thus, the extent to which firms are less or more environmentally conscious is captured via a smaller or larger δ', respectively.

higher output as products become more differentiated) and a relatively large δ' helps offset increased emissions via lower abatement costs. If δ' is somewhat small then environmentally conscious firms partially offset increased emissions, but emissions still rise as products become more differentiated i.e., $e_\gamma < 0$, if $\delta' \leq \delta(n-1)/D$.

Proposition 1. *(a) Industry emissions fall as products become more differentiated if and only if firms are sufficiently environmentally conscious and pollution-moderate (i.e., $\delta' > \delta(\alpha - \tilde{c} - \delta\tau)(n-1)/D(\alpha - \tilde{c} - 2\delta\tau)$). (b) If δ' is somewhat small (i.e., $\delta' \leq \delta(n-1)/D$), then environmentally conscious firms partially offset increased emissions, but emissions still rise as products become more differentiated i.e., $e_\gamma < 0$.*

Proposition 1(a) suggests that as products become more differentiated industry emissions may fall by more for initially small values of γ, which are associated with small values of δ. Formally, under proposition 1(a) $e_\gamma > 0$ and $e_{\gamma\gamma} < 0$ where subscripts denote first and second order partial derivatives. The intuition is that for initially small values of γ (and therefore small values of δ) any increase in emissions, arising from higher output as products become more differentiated, is offset by a small intensity coefficient; at the same time, a large value of δ' indicates that emissions fall with more differentiated products since firms are sufficiently environmentally conscious. In the case where firms are not environmentally conscious (i.e., $\delta' \simeq 0$) emissions rise by more as products become more differentiated since (i) firms are not taking any steps to lower emissions via the intensity coefficient and (ii) output rises rapidly at initially small values of γ as product become more differentiated; formally, $e_\gamma < 0$ and $e_{\gamma\gamma} > 0$ (see the appendix for a derivation). These results illustrate the important role of abatement via changes in the degree of product differentiation.

Proposition 2. *If firms are sufficiently environmentally conscious (i.e., $\delta' > \delta(\alpha - \tilde{c} - \delta\tau)(n-1)/D(\alpha - \tilde{c} - 2\delta\tau)$), then emissions are more likely to fall by more at initially small values of γ. Alternatively, if firms are not sufficiently conscious ($\delta' \simeq 0$), then emissions are more likely to rise for initially small γ.*

4. Optimal Policy

The government chooses the emission tax,τ, through welfare maximization. In particular, the government solves

$$\max_{\tau} W = CS + ne\tau + n\pi - \varphi(en) \tag{6}$$

where CS denotes consumer surplus, and the function φ represents the damage from pollution satisfying $\varphi' > 0$ and $\varphi'' > 0$. Optimal policy is thus characterized by the following first-order condition (subscripts denote partial derivatives):

$$\begin{aligned} \frac{1}{n} W_\tau &= \beta q q_\tau - (\varphi' - \tau) e_\tau = 0 \\ &= -\delta\beta q/D + (\varphi'^2/D) = 0 \end{aligned} \tag{7}$$

There are two effects which the government needs to balance, namely, the output distortion and the damage from pollution. It is easy to show that the optimal tax is set below marginal damages in order to address the output distortion since $e_\tau < 0$ and $q_\tau < 0$. Additionally, evaluating (7) at $\tau = 0$ and using the strict concavity assumption of the $W(\cdot)$ function, indicates that the optimal tax is positive if the abatement effect is large; that is, if the incentives of the tax to induce abatement are sufficiently strong. Formally, at $\tau = 0$ $W_\tau > 0$ if φ'/z is large. In this case optimal policy is taxation even when the government cares about addressing the output distortion vis-à-vis damages to the environment, thereby ruling out the possibility of subsidizing output (i.e., negative optimal emission tax) because of the role of abatement.[4] To see this result consider, as in Fujiwara (2009), a damage function so that $\varphi' = en$.[5] The closed-form solution for the optimal emission tax is then given by

$$\tau^* = \frac{(\alpha - \tilde{c})\delta\left(Dn/z - \beta + \delta^2 n\right)}{\delta^2\left(Dn/z - \beta + \delta^2 n\right) + D^2/z + D\delta^2 + (Dn/z)(D/z + \delta^2)} \tag{8}$$

where $\tau^* > 0$ *if and only if* $Dn/z - \beta + n\delta^2 > 0$ and $D = 2\beta + \gamma(n-1) > 0$. The term Dn/z captures the abatement induced by the tax (see equation 5)

[4] A large optimal tax in the presence of abatement is also pointed out by Ebert (1992, p.161).

[5] Strictly speaking Fujiwara's model assumes $\delta = 1$, $1/z = 0$ and $\varphi = sne$. Equation (8) is equivalent to Fujiwara's under these two assumptions, plus $s = 1$.

and β the output distortion. Intuitively, the tax is positive to tackle the damage from pollution via higher induced abatement and production costs, and set below marginal damages to address the output distortion. This result, however, contrasts with Fujiwara (2009) where abatement efforts are assumed away. In the present analysis Fujiwara's result is a special case and so it is obtained if $1/z \simeq 0$ i.e., abatement efforts are negligible. In the special case where $z = 1$, then the optimal tax is unambiguously positive.

Proposition 3. *Let $\varphi' = en$. In the presence of sufficiently large induced pollution abatement, (i.e., $Dn/z > \beta - n\delta^2$), optimal policy is taxation.*

Next, the effect of product differentiation on policy is examined. As a first case, it is noteworthy that if $\delta = 1$, $\delta' = 0$ and $1/z \simeq 0$, then identical results to Fujiwara (2009) are obtained through differentiation of (8) with respect to γ. In order to examine the role of abatement efforts it is useful to differentiate $W_\tau(\tau(\gamma), \gamma) = 0$, which yields $-W_{\tau\tau} d\tau/d\gamma = W_{\tau\gamma}$ where $W_{\tau\tau} < 0$:

$$n^{-1} W_{\tau\gamma} = (\varphi' - \tau)\frac{(n-1)}{zD} + \beta q_\tau q_\gamma - \varphi'' e_\tau \delta q_\gamma$$

$$+ \delta' \left(\frac{\delta(\varphi' - \tau)}{D} - \varphi'' e_\tau q - \frac{(\varphi' - \tau)}{z\delta} \right) \tag{9}$$

where from (7) $W_{\tau\gamma}$ is the direct effect of γ (i.e., for given tax) and $\beta q - \delta(\varphi' - \tau) = (\varphi' - \tau)D/z\delta > 0$, and $e_\tau < 0$, $q_\tau < 0$, $q_\gamma < 0$. The first term in (9) is positive because of the presence of pollution abatement; that is, because of pollution abatement by firms the government can afford a reduction in the optimal tax as products become differentiated to address the output distortion arising from the increased market power by firms. The second term, $\beta q_\tau q_\gamma$, is the profit effect which is positive since a lower tax raises profits; and the third term, $-\varphi'' \delta e_\tau q_\gamma$, is negative thus indicating that the government needs to address higher pollution arising from the increase in output as products become more differentiated. The last three terms (i.e., the terms in $\delta'(\cdot)$) capture the effects via firms differentiating themselves as environmentally conscious firms. In particular, the first two terms are positive which indicates that the government can afford a reduction in the tax due to the reduction in emissions by firms via δ' i.e., lower emissions via abatement from environmentally conscious firms. The last term is negative and captures the increased emissions arising from lower production costs and therefore higher output as firms differentiate themselves.

As a benchmark case where $\delta' = 0$ and $1/z \simeq 0$ (i.e., no abatement) the tax falls *if and only if* the government puts more weight on the output distortion (i.e., $\beta - \varphi''\delta > 0$); this is analogous to results in the literature. In the case where $1/z \neq 0$ and $\delta' = 0$, the tax falls with more differentiated products (decrease in γ) *if and only if* $1/z$ is large even if the government puts enough weight on environmental damages ($\beta - \varphi''\delta < 0$).[6] This result illustrates the role of abatement, in particular the incentives for abatement the tax induces, which affords the government a tax reduction, to address the output distortion arising from more differentiated markets, even when damages to the environment are sufficiently important. Indeed, even if $1/z$ is not large enough the government still gains some room to lower the tax to address the output distortion and so the emission tax is likely to increase by less in the case where the government cares about damages to the environment.

Next, consider the case where $1/z \simeq 0$, $\delta' \neq 0$. In this case the optimal tax falls via firms being more environmentally conscious and the promotion of profits, but rises as more emissions take place as products become more differentiated. If the effect which takes place via firms being more environmentally conscious is large (i.e., $\delta' > \delta(\alpha - \tilde{c} - \delta\tau)(n-1)/D(\alpha - \tilde{c} - 2\delta\tau)$), then the tax falls even as the government cares a lot about environmental damages; this is because the reduction in emissions, which takes place as firms become environmentally conscious, affords the government a reduction in the tax to encourage output and profits.

Proposition 4. *Let $1/z \simeq 0$, $\delta' \neq 0$. Then, if firms are sufficiently environmentally conscious (i.e., $\delta' \geq \delta(\alpha - \tilde{c} - \delta\tau)(n-1)/D(\alpha - \tilde{c} - 2\delta\tau)$), then the optimal tax falls with more differentiated products even as the government cares a lot about environmental damages.*

If the effect via δ' is rather small (i.e., firms are not necessarily very environmentally conscious in the sense that $\delta' < \delta(\alpha - \tilde{c} - \delta\tau)(n-1)/D(\alpha - \tilde{c} - 2\delta\tau)$) and the government cares more about the output distortion vis-à-vis damages from pollution (i.e., $\varphi''\delta$ is small), then the tax falls as γ falls; the tax rises if the government cares sufficiently about the environment (i.e., $\varphi''\delta$ is large). In

[6] Since $z > 1$, $1/z \in (0, 1)$ and so we shall assume that the condition of large $1/z$ is consistent with these bounds. Formally, from (9) simplification in this case yields a polynomial of degree two in $1/z$. In any case, the presence of $1/z > 0$ ensures that the government is likely to increase the tax by less as products become more differentiated.

particular, if $1/z \simeq 0$, $\delta' \neq 0$ then using (7) the expression in (9) becomes

$$Dn^{-1}W_{\tau\gamma} = -\delta q_\gamma(\beta - \varphi''\delta) + \delta' q(\beta + \varphi''\delta)$$

$$= \delta\varphi'' e_\gamma + \beta(\delta' q - \delta q_\gamma) \quad (10)$$

where $q_\gamma < 0$ and as indicated in proposition 1(a) $e_\gamma = \delta q_\gamma + \delta' q < 0$ *if and only if* $\delta' < \delta(\alpha - \tilde{c} - \delta\tau)(n-1)/D(\alpha - \tilde{c} - 2\delta\tau)$ where $\alpha - \tilde{c} - 2\delta\tau > 0$.

Proposition 5. *In the absence of abatement efforts, the optimal tax rises if and only if the government cares sufficiently about the environment. However, in the presence of sufficient pollution abatement efforts by firms either directly (i.e., via $1/z$) or by differentiating themselves as environmentally conscious (i.e., via δ'), then the optimal tax may fall as products become differentiated even as the government cares sufficiently about environmental damages (i.e., $\beta < \varphi''\delta$).*

In the case where there is some form of abatement both directly and via differentiation (i.e., $1/z \neq 0$ and $\delta' \neq 0$) there is a myriad of cases so here we point a few. For a range of δ' the extent to which the optimal tax may decrease or increase as products become more differentiated depends on whether the government puts sufficient weight on environmental damages. In particular, (9) can be re-written as follows:

$$Dn^{-1}W_{\tau\gamma} = \frac{\varphi' - \tau}{\delta}\left(-\delta'/z + \frac{\delta(n-1)}{zD} + \delta^2\delta'\right) + \beta q_\gamma q_\tau - \varphi'' e_\tau e_\gamma \quad (11)$$

where the first two terms vanish if $\delta(\alpha - \tilde{c} - \delta\tau)(n-1)/D(\alpha - \tilde{c} - 2\delta\tau) > \delta(n-1)/D = \delta'$, the last term is negative since $e_\tau < 0$ and $e_\gamma < 0$, and the remaining terms are positive. Intuitively, for small δ' abatement efforts by firms are partially offset (i.e., $e_\gamma < 0$) and so the government still needs to balance damages to the environment. If φ'' is small then the tax falls as products become more differentiated.

If $\delta' \geq \delta(\alpha - \tilde{c} - \delta\tau)(n-1)/D(\alpha - \tilde{c} - 2\delta\tau)$, then the last term in (11) vanishes as firms differentiate themselves sufficiently in the sense that there is no need to adjust the tax upwards via this effect (i.e., $e_\gamma \geq 0$); the first and third terms in parentheses are negative and positive, respectively, thus indicating that the increase in emissions is tackled via a higher tax but also output is encouraged through less taxation. If this latter effect is large enough($1/z \leq \delta^2$), then the optimal tax falls. Intuitively, on the one hand, as firms take on sufficient abatement via product differentiation, δ', emissions do not rise as much so there is less need for a tax increase with more differentiated products; on the other, with insufficient direct abatement, $1/z \leq \delta^2$, the increase in emissions, arising from the room the government has to afford a tax reduction due to abatement efforts, $1/z$, is less which in turn suggests that there is less need for a tax increase.

Proposition 6. *Let $1/z \neq 0$, $\delta' \neq 0$. Then, if firms take on sufficient abatement as environmentally conscious firms (i.e., $\delta' \geq \delta(\alpha - \tilde{c} - \delta\tau)(n-1)/D(\alpha - \tilde{c} - 2\delta\tau)$) and relatively less direct abatement (i.e., $1/z \leq \delta^2$), then the optimal tax falls with more differentiated products.*

5. Product Differentiation and Industry Emissions

This section looks at the change in industry emissions as products become more differentiated both via the tax adjustment and the direct effect. One of the main policy implications derived in this section is that industry emissions may still rise even as the government adjusts the optimal tax in order to balance the output distortion and damages from pollution. It is also shown that in some cases industry emissions may fall even as the government lowers the tax since, among others, firms become sufficiently environmentally conscious. We shall consider some of the results from previous sections and differentiation of $e(\tau(\gamma), \gamma)$, which gives

$$de/d\gamma = e_\tau \tau_\gamma + e_\gamma \tag{12}$$

where the first term captures the effect via the tax adjustment and $e_\tau < 0$, and the second term, e_γ, the direct effect (i.e., for given tax). Let $1/z \simeq 0$ and $\delta' = 0$ as a first benchmark case (i.e., no abatement). In this case the last term in (12) is negative and $\tau_\gamma > 0$ *if and only if* the government weighs the output distortion sufficiently, and as a result industry emissions rise with more differentiated products. Intuitively, since the government lowers the tax to address the output distortion emissions rise via the tax and, additionally, for a given tax emissions also rise because of an increase in output as product become differentiated. This result suggests that in the absence of abatement efforts an additional policy (e.g., output subsidy) may be needed to address the output distortion and at the same time tackle higher emissions. In contrast, if the government cares about damages to the environment then the tax rises with more differentiated products and, as a result, emissions fall via the tax; emissions still rise via the direct effect. Thus, industry emissions fall *if and only if* the effect via the tax is sufficiently strong (i.e., $-\delta q_\tau(\beta - \delta^2\varphi'')/nW_{\tau\tau} > 1$ where $\beta < \delta^2\varphi''$).[7] In particular, in the benchmark case where $1/z \simeq 0$ and $\delta' = 0$ total change in emissions is given by

$$\frac{de}{d\gamma} = \frac{-q_\gamma \delta}{D}\left(\frac{-\delta q_\tau(\beta - \delta^2\varphi'')}{nW_{\tau\tau}} - 1\right) \tag{13}$$

where $W_{\tau\tau} < 0$, $q_\tau < 0$, $q_\gamma < 0$, $D = 2\beta + \gamma(n-1) > 0$. As a second case, if $1/z \neq 0$ and $\delta' = 0$ then the tax falls as products become more differentiated with sufficient abatement (i.e., $1/z$ large) and emissions still rise via the direct effect. As a result, industry emissions rise as products become more differentiated. If instead the abatement effect is small analogous results to (13) are obtained.

Next, suppose that $1/z \simeq 0$, $\delta' \neq 0$, $\delta' < \delta(\alpha - \tilde{c} - \delta\tau)(n-1)/D(\alpha - \tilde{c} - 2\delta\tau)$. In this case emissions rise via the direct effect, the tax may rise or fall and so emissions may rise or fall via the tax. If damages are not important (i.e., $\varphi''\delta$ is small) then the tax falls as products become more differentiated thereby raising emissions. As a result, industry emissions rise with more differentiated products. This result indicates that if firms are not very environmentally conscious, then industry emissions rise if the government does not care sufficiently about pollution damages. In particular, using (12) and (10) gives

$$\frac{de}{d\gamma} = -e_\gamma\left(\frac{\delta q_\tau \varphi''}{W_{\tau\tau}} - 1\right) - e_\tau \frac{\beta(\delta' q - \delta q_\gamma)}{W_{\tau\tau}} < 0 \ if \ \delta q_\tau \varphi''/W_{\tau\tau} < 1 \tag{14}$$

where $e_\gamma < 0$. In the special case where $\delta' = \delta(\alpha - \tilde{c} - \delta\tau)(n-1)/D(\alpha - \tilde{c} - 2\delta\tau)$ and $1/z \simeq 0$ the direct effect is negligible and the tax falls with more differentiated products and, as a result, industry emissions rise unambiguously. If $\delta' > \delta(\alpha - \tilde{c} - \delta\tau)(n-1)/D(\alpha - \tilde{c} - 2\delta\tau)$, then the direct effect is positive and the tax falls with more differentiated products; therefore, industry emissions may fall if the adjustment in the tax is small.

Proposition 7. *Industry emissions rise if firms take on sufficient abatement effort directly i.e., $1/z$ is large. If sufficient abatement efforts are taken via differentiation i.e., δ' is large, then industry emissions may fall if the tax adjustment is small.*

[7] Industry emissions are given by $E = ne$. Since n is fixed, results in this section apply to industry emissions.

Proposition 7 suggests that the presence of abatement increases the likelihood of increased industry emissions in a number of cases; this is because in the presence of abatement the government is more likely to afford a tax reduction to address the output distortion as products become more differentiated. This in turn indicates the need for additional policies, even in the presence of abatement efforts, if lower industry emissions are to be achieved in the case where changes in the degree of product differentiation take place. Additionally, policies to encourage/discourage either type of abatement may also aid to achieve the objective of lowering industry emissions.

Conclusion

This chapter examines the role of abatement efforts by firms in the characterization of the optimal emission tax as products become more differentiated. The analysis becomes relevant particularly since across a variety of industries firms are taking steps to differentiate themselves as environmentally conscious. As a result, policymakers should adapt environmental policy to this changing business environment in order to address environmental damages and potential market distortions. Surprisingly, the literature on environmental policy in the presence of horizontal product differentiation and abatement efforts has put only partial attention to this issue. The analysis indicates that in the presence of abatement efforts by firms the government may afford a tax reduction as products become more differentiated. This result is important because it illustrates the role abatement efforts may have in allowing the government to address the output distortion, an issue which is prevalent in a number of imperfectly competitive industries. This adjustment in the tax, however, may lead to an increase in industry emissions, which in turn raises the question of potential policies which may be implemented along with the emission tax. In this regard, the analysis indicates that policies which may encourage firms to differentiate themselves as environmentally conscious firms may aid in the reduction of industry emissions and at the same time allow a reduction in the emission tax.

The results and policy implications presented in this chapter are inevitably limited to the assumptions made about the functional forms of the cost function, fixed number of firms and strategic behavior of firms. As a result, there are several lines of research which may be explored. First, the case of free entry and exit of firms may be considered as a potentially interesting case, particularly in industries where entry costs are relatively small. Second, the assumption about exogenous changes in the degree of product differentiation could be relaxed. Although the literature has explored this issue in the context of vertically differentiated markets (e.g., Bansal and Gangopadhyay, 2003; Conrad, 2005; Rodríguez-Ibeas, 2006), the present model set-up could be extended to include consumer heterogeneity. As mentioned earlier, the analysis indicates that additional policies may be needed to complement the emission tax and, as a result, the model could incorporate additional policies such as subsidies (as in e.g., Poyago-Theotoky, 2003; McGinty and de Vries, 2009). Since a key aspect of the chapter is the presence abatement efforts, an extension of the model may include more general functional forms for the cost function as long as the abatement component remains tractable throughout the model.

A. Appendix

Here we derive equation (7). The welfare function, $W(\cdot)$, is given in equation (6) i.e., $W = CS(Q) + ne\tau + n\pi - \varphi(en)$. Then, the derivative of W with respect to τ is given by

$$W_\tau = -nqp_\tau + n\pi_\tau + (\tau - \varphi')ne_\tau + ne$$

where it is well known that $dCS = -Qdp$. Factoring out n gives

$$\frac{1}{n}W_\tau = -qp_\tau + \pi_\tau + (\tau - \varphi')e_\tau + e \tag{A.1}$$

Next, we find the expression for π_τ. Profits are given by

$$\pi = pq - \tilde{c}q - z(\delta q - e)^2/2 - e\tau - f \tag{A.2}$$

where $\delta q - e = a = \tau/z$ from the first order condition in equation (3). Using $e_\tau = \delta q_\tau - a_\tau = \delta q_\tau - 1/z$, the derivative of (A.2) with respect to τ yields

$$\begin{aligned}\pi_\tau &= (p - \tilde{c} - \delta\tau)q_\tau - \tau/z - e + \tau/z + qp_\tau \\ &= (p - \tilde{c} - \delta\tau)q_\tau - e + qp_\tau \end{aligned} \tag{A.3}$$

where $p - \tilde{c} - \delta\tau = \beta q$ from the first order conditions given by equations 2 and 3. Hence, (A.3) can be re-written as

$$\pi_\tau = \beta qq_\tau - e + qp_\tau \tag{A.4}$$

Substituting (A.4) into (A.1) and simplifying gives equation (7).

Next, we derive the condition for e_γ to be negative or positive. In particular, from (5)

$$e_\gamma = \frac{\delta'}{D}(Dq - \delta\tau) - \frac{\delta q(n-1)}{D}$$
$$= \frac{\delta'(\alpha - \tilde{c} - 2\delta\tau)}{D} - \frac{\delta(\alpha - \tilde{c} - \delta\tau)(n-1)}{D^2} \tag{A.5}$$

Hence,

$$e_\gamma > 0 \Leftrightarrow \delta' > \frac{\delta(n-1)(\alpha - \tilde{c} - \delta\tau)}{(\alpha - \tilde{c} - 2\delta\tau)D} \tag{A.6}$$

where $D = 2\beta + \gamma(n-1)$ and by assumption $(\alpha - \tilde{c} - 2\delta\tau) > 0$. If $\delta' \simeq 0$, then $e_\gamma < 0$. Next, we derive the expression for $e_{\gamma\gamma}$. Differentiation of e_γ in (5) w.r.t. γ gives

$$e_{\gamma\gamma} = \frac{2\delta(n-1)^2 q}{D^2} + \frac{2\delta'}{D}\left(-q(n-1) - \tau\delta' + \frac{\delta\tau(n-1)}{D}\right) \tag{A.7}$$

If δ is small and δ' large (i.e., $\delta' > \delta(n-1)(\alpha - \tilde{c} - \delta\tau)/(\alpha - \tilde{c} - 2\delta\tau)D)$, then $e_{\gamma\gamma} < 0$. If $\delta' \simeq 0$ then $e_{\gamma\gamma} > 0$. □

References

[1] Cellini, R., Lambertini, L., Ottaviano, G.I.P. (2004) Welfare in a differentiated oligopoly with free entry: a cautionary note. *Research in Economics*, 58, 125-133.

[2] Carlsson, F. (2000). Environmental taxation and strategic commitment in duopoly models. *Environmental & Resource Economics*, 15 (3), 243-256.

[3] Bansal, S., & Gangopadhyay, S. (2003). Tax/subsidy policies in the presence of environmentally aware consumers. *Journal of Environmental Economics and Management*, 45 (2), 333-355.

[4] Conrad, K. (2005). Price competition and product differentiation when consumers care for the environment. *Environmental & Resource Economics*, 31, 1-19.

[5] Ebert, U. (1992). Pigouvian tax and market structure: The case of oligopoly and different abatement technologies. *FinanzArchiv/Public Finance Analysis*, 49 (2), 154-166.

[6] Eriksson, C. (2004). Can green consumerism replace environmental regulation? - a differentiated-products example. *Resource and Energy Economics*, 26, 281-293.

[7] Espínola-Arredondo, A., & Zhao, H. (2012). Environmental policy in a linear city model of product differentiation. *Environment and Development Economics*, 17 (4), 461â€“477.

[8] Fujiwara, K. (2009). Environmental policies in a differentiated oligopoly revisited. *Resource and Energy Economics*, 31, 239-247.

[9] Gautier, L. (2013). Multilateral policy reform of emission taxes and abatement subsidies in a two-country model with oligopolistic interdependence. *Environmental Economics and Policy Studies*, 15 (1), 59-71.

[10] Katsoulacos, Y., & Xepapadeas, A. (1995). Environmental policy under oligopoly with endogenous market structure. *Scandinavian Journal of Economics*, 97 (3), 411-420.

[11] Lahiri, S., & Symeonidis, G. (2007). Piecemeal multilateral environmental policy reforms under asymmetric oligopoly. *Journal of Public Economic Theory*, 9 (5), 885-899.

[12] Lee, S.H. (1999). Optimal taxation for polluting oligopolists with endogenous market structure. *Journal of Regulatory Economics*, 15, 293-308.

[13] Lambertini, L. (2013) *Oligopoly, the environment and natural resources*. London: Routledge. .

[14] Levine, D. (1985). Taxation within Cournot oligopoly. *Journal of Public Economics*, 27, 281-290.

[15] Lyon, T.P., & Maxwell, J.W. (2008). Corporate social responsibility and the environment: A theoretical perspective. *Review of Environmental Economics and Policy*, 2(2), 240-260.

[16] McGinty, M., & de Vries, F.P. (2009). Technology diffusion, product differentiation and environmental subsidies. *B.E. Journal of Economic Analysis and Policy: Topics in Economic Analysis and Policy*, 9(1), 1-25.

[17] Montero, P. (2002a). Permits, standards, and technology innovation. *Journal of Environmental Economics and Management*, 44(1), 23-44.

[18] Montero, P. (2002b). Market structure and environmental innovation. *Journal of Applied Economics*, 5(2), 293-325.

[19] Portney, P.R. (2008). The (not so) new corporate social responsibility: An empirical perspective. *Review of Environmental Economics and Policy*, 2(2), 261-275.

[20] Poyago-Theotoky, J. (2003). Optimal environmental taxation, R&D subsidization and the role of market conduct. *Finnish Economic Papers*, 16(1), 15-26.

[21] Requate, T. (2006). Environmental policy under imperfect competition. In T. Tietenberg, & H. Folmer (Eds.) *The international yearbook of environmental and resource economics 2006/2007* (pp. 120-207). UK: Edward Elgar Publishing Limited.

[22] Rodríguez-Ibeas, R. (2006). Environmental product differentiation and environmental awareness. *Environmental & Resource Economics*, 36(2), 237-254.

[23] Simpson, R.D. (1995). Optimal pollution taxation in a Cournot duopoly. *Environmental and Resource Economics*, 6, 359-369.

[24] Thollander, P., & Ottosson, M. (2008). An energy efficient Swedish pulp and paper industry â€“ exploring barriers to and driving forces for cost-effective energy efficiency investments. *Energy Efficiency*, 1(1), 21-34.

[25] US Economics and Statistics Administration (2010). *US Carbon dioxide emissions and intensities over time: A detailed accounting of industries, government and households.* http://www.esa.doc.gov/sites/default/files/reports/documents/co2reportfinal.pdf

[26] Ulph, A., & Ulph, D. (1996). Trade, strategic innovation and strategic environmental policy â€“ a general analysis. In C. Carraro, Y. Katsoulacos

& A. Xepapadeas (Eds.), *Environmental Policy and Market Structure* (pp. 181-208). Netherlands: Kluwer Academic Publishers.

[27] Ulph, A., & Ulph, D. (2007). Climate change-environmental and technology policies in a strategic context. *Environmental & Resource Economics*, 37(1), 159-180.

[28] Yakita, A., & Yamauchi, H. (2011). Environmental awareness and environmental R&D spillovers in differentiated duopoly. *Research Economics*, 65, 137-143.

In: Economics of Environmental Policy ... ISBN: 978-1-63463-165-5
Editors: M. G. Fikru and M. Insall

Chapter 2

THE INTERPLAY BETWEEN PROFIT AND ENVIRONMENTAL TAXATION: INCENTIVES TO CREATE RJVS FOR GREEN INNOVATIONS*

***Davide Dragone*[1], *Luca Lambertini*[1,†] *and Arsen Palestini*[2]**
[1]Department of Economics, University of Bologna, Bologna, Italy
[2]MEMOTEF, University of Rome "La Sapienza", Roma, Italy

Abstract

We consider the joint effect of profit and emission taxation in a model of imperfect competition with environmental externalities. We show that, when both profit taxation and emission taxation are used, the former is no longer neutral. The two fiscal tools are substitutes, and for any profit taxation rate there exists a unique optimal environmental tax rate that entails the first best outcome as an equilibrium. Our analysis therefore suggests that policy makers in charge of different taxation policies should coordinate in order to optimally design the tax menu for firms. Conversely, profit taxation has no consequences on firms' green R&D efforts for the attainment of abatement technologies. In this regard, we also show that independent R&D projects accompanied by information sharing (i.e., technological spillovers) outperform a joint venture when a green innovation is at stake.

*We would like to thank two anonymous referees and the Editor for precious comments and suggestions on a previous draft. The usual disclaimer applies.

†E-mail address: luca.lambertini@unibo.it; Fax: +39-051-2092664 (Corresponding Author)

JEL Codes: H23, H25, L13, O31, Q51

Keywords: Externalities, Pigouvian taxation, oligopoly

1. Introduction

There exists a relatively large amount of literature on profit taxation in static models of imperfect competition (Levin, 1985; Besley, 1989; Delipalla and Keen, 1992; Dung, 1993; Denicolò and Matteuzzi, 2000; Ushio, 2000, *inter alia*). A well established result of this literature is that the taxation of operative profits (defined as the profits gross of fixed costs) is neutral, in that it does not affect first order conditions on market variables.

A parallel stream of research focuses on the effectiveness of emission taxation in inducing firms to internalize the externalities involved in the production process (Benchekroun and Long, 1998, 2002; Karp and Livernois, 1994; Katsoulacos and Xepapadeas, 1995; Damania, 1996, *inter alia*). The effect of this form of taxation is to modify the incentives for the firm in order to make the choice of its market variable consistent with the outcome that maximizes social welfare.

The interplay between environmental taxation and other forms of taxation is also discussed in the literature. In particular, a general equilibrium approach is used to investigate the optimal design of an emissions tax used in an economic system where other *distortionary* taxes already exist.[1]

In this paper we consider the possibility, to the best of our knowledge overlooked so far, that the adoption of environmental taxation may cause preexisting taxation to switch from neutral to distortionary. To this aim, we examine the joint effect of profit and emission taxation in a partial equilibrium model of oligopolistic competition *à la* Cournot. We show that, when both profit taxation and emission taxation are being used, the former is no longer neutral. The two fiscal tools behave as substitutes, and for any profit tax rate there exists a unique optimal emission tax rate that entails the first best outcome as an equilibrium. This prompts for a coordination effort among the policy makers in charge of designing optimally the different tax rates to which firms are subject

[1]This issue has generated a lively debate on the feasibility and efficiency of carbon and energy taxes, emission permits and performance standards. See Bovenberg and Goulder (1996), Cremer *et al.* (1998), Goulder *et al.* (1997), Parry (1997), Goulder *et al.* (1999), Parry and Williams (1999), Fullerton and Metcalf (2001), to mention only a few.

in industries featuring environmental externalities.

We also extend the perspective to encompass the possibility that firms invest in R&D aimed at attaining cleaner technologies as a result of emission taxation. *A priori*, the coexistence of profit and emission taxation may lead one to think that the resulting green technological improvements will be lower than they would in the case in which profit taxation were assumed away, as any additional fiscal pressure hinders profits and therefore makes it more difficult for firms to cover R&D costs. Indeed, the opposite emerges at the subgame perfect equilibrium, as profit taxation only affects output decisions. Additionally, we investigate the choice between fully non cooperative behavior (admitting the possibility of technological spillovers among firms) and a joint venture with cost sharing and full spillovers. The outcome of this part of the analysis speaks openly in favour of information sharing across independent ventures, as a joint venture would lead the industry to shrink the overall effort towards the attainment of green technologies via the familiar cost-reducing argument associated with the use of a single R&D lab.

2. Profit Taxation is Not Neutral

Consider a market with demand function $p = p(Q)$, with $p(Q)$ decreasing and non-convex in Q, where Q is aggregate output. Production costs for each firm $i = 1, 2, ...n$ are given by $C_i = C(q_i) + f$, with $\partial C(q_i)/\partial q_i > 0$ and the fixed cost $f > 0$. The latter is taken to be small enough to ensure that individual profits be non-negative at the Cournot equilibrium with n firms. Supplying the final good to the market entails a negative externality $S = S(Q)$, where $Q = \sum_{i=1}^{n} q_i$, with $\partial S(Q)/\partial Q > 0$ and $\partial S(Q)/\partial q_i > 0$ for all $i = 1, 2, ...n$.[2] Let $\theta \geq 0$ be the uniform tax rate to be paid by each firm on the volume of emissions, and let $t \in [0, 1)$ be the tax rate on operative profits defined as $\widehat{\pi}_i = p(Q)q_i - C(q_i)$, i.e., excluding the fixed cost component and the environmental tax.[3] This implies that the firm's profit is

$$\pi_i(Q) = [p(Q)q_i - C(q_i)]\,(1 - t) - f - \theta S(Q) \geq 0 \tag{1}$$

[2] A similar reasoning holds when the externality is positive, provided the signs are changed to take into account the introduction of a subsidy.

[3] Hence, this model is largely the same as in Katsoulacos and Xepapadeas (1995), except for the presence of taxation applied onto operative profits.

If firms compete à *la* Cournot-Nash, the first order condition for each firm i is

$$\frac{\partial \pi_i}{\partial q_i} = \left[\frac{\partial p(Q)}{\partial q_i} q_i + p(Q) - \frac{\partial C(q_i)}{\partial q_i}\right](1-t) - \theta \frac{\partial S(Q)}{\partial q_i} = 0 \qquad (2)$$

which identifies a maximum if

$$\frac{\partial^2 p(Q)}{\partial q_i^2} < \frac{\theta \partial^2 S(Q)/\partial q_i^2}{(1-t)\, q_i} + \frac{1}{q_i}\left[\frac{\partial^2 C(q_i)}{\partial q_i^2} - 2\frac{\partial p(Q)}{\partial q_i}\right] \qquad (3)$$

Clearly, when $\theta = 0$, the choice of the tax rate on profit is irrelevant as the optimal level of individual output is not affected by t (see equation (2))[4]. Nevertheless, this conclusion no longer holds if θ is positive.

Lemma 1. *Provided firms are subject to any tax rate $\theta > 0$ on polluting emissions, then profit taxation is non-neutral.*

Define as $q_i^*(t, \theta)$ the solution to (2). Then, using the implicit function theorem, one can examine the effect of the taxation menu on the optimal output of each individual firm, as well as the interplay between the two forms of taxation, to prove:

Proposition 1. *In correspondence of the optimal output decision of the generic firm i, emission taxation and profit taxation are strategic substitutes.*

Proof. It suffices to observe that

$$\frac{d\theta}{dt} = -\frac{\partial^2 \pi_i}{\partial q_i \partial t} \Big/ \frac{\partial^2 \pi_i}{\partial q_i \partial \theta} = -\frac{q_i \cdot \partial p(Q)/\partial q_i + p(Q) - \partial C(q_i)/\partial q_i}{\partial S(Q)/\partial q_i} < 0 \qquad (4)$$

because the numerator is necessarily positive from (2). Hence the tax menu available to the policy maker(s) is characterized by a negative marginal rate of substitution between the two forms of taxation. ■

[4]The case in which $\frac{\partial S(Q)}{\partial q_i} = 0$ is not interesting, as this implies that the firm has no influence on the externality.

3. Example

Consider an oligopolistic market where n symmetric firms produce a homogeneous good. The market demand function is $p = a - Q$ where $Q \equiv \sum_{i=1}^{n} q_i$ and q_i is firm i's output$_i$, $i = 1, 2, ...n$. Technology is the same for all firms and it is summarized by the cost function $C(q_i) = cq_i - f$, where $c \geq 0$. This entails that firm i's net profits in absence of any taxation are $\pi_i = (p - c)\, q_i - f$.

Supplying the final good entails a negative environmental externality $S = \sum_{i=1}^{N} bq_i$, with $b \geq 0$, that negatively affects consumers' utility. The social planner chooses the Pigouvian tax rate $\theta \geq 0$ that each firm has to pay as a function of the amount of the environmental externality produced by the industry. Moreover, operative profits are taxed at the rate $t \in [0, 1)$, so that the net after-tax profits of firm i are

$$\pi_i = (p - c)\, q_i(1 - t) - f - \theta S \tag{5}$$

The present game has a two-stage structure: in the first stage, the social planner chooses the taxation rate on profits t and the taxation rate on the negative externality θ produced by the industry in order to maximize the social welfare function

$$SW = n\pi_i + CS \tag{6}$$

where SW stands for *social welfare.* Total tax revenues, $T = n\left[(p - c)\, q_i t + \theta S\right]$ are transferred to consumers, whose surplus reads as

$$CS = \frac{Q^2}{2} - S + T \tag{7}$$

where CS stands for *consumer surplus.* In the second stage, firms compete *à la* Cournot-Nash.

4. Equilibrium Analysis

The solution concept is subgame perfection by backward induction. This requires determining the optimal output produced by each firm as a function of the taxes chosen by the social planner as the leader in the first stage. From the first order condition at the second stage, one obtains:

$$q_i^*(t, \theta) = \frac{1}{1+n}\left(a - c - \frac{b\theta}{1-t}\right) \tag{8}$$

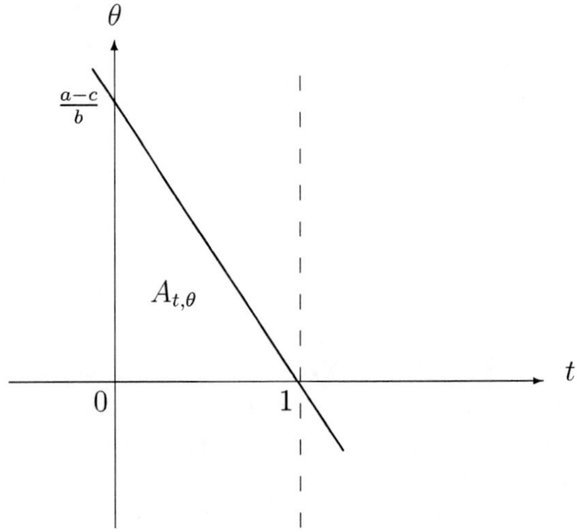

Figure 1. Region $A_{t,\theta}$.

for every $i = 1, 2, ...n$. Expression (8) is positive in the following subset of the admissible tax rate plane:

$$A_{t,\theta} := \left\{ (t, \theta) \mid 0 \leq \theta < \frac{(a-c)(1-t)}{b}, \ 0 \leq t < 1 \right\} \tag{9}$$

Region $A_{t,\theta}$ is represented in Figure 1.

As $\partial q_i(t, \theta)/\partial t < 0$ for all $\theta > 0$ and $\partial q_i(t, \theta)/\partial \theta < 0$ for all $t \in [0, 1)$, we can state the following:

Lemma 2. *For $\theta > 0$, the individual output level decreases (increases) if the taxation rate on operative profits and on the environmental externality increases (decreases).*

Note also that, if the social planner does not tax the environmental externality, then the tax rate on variable profits does not affect the optimal individual output.

Substituting (8) in (5) yields the following expressions for the net individual profits, the amount of externality and total revenues:

$$\pi_i^* = \frac{(1-t)\left[(a-c)^2(1-t) - f(1+n)^2\right] - b\theta\left[(a-c)(1+n^2)(1-t) + bn^2\theta\right]}{(1+n)^2(1-t)} \tag{10}$$

$$S^* = \frac{nb}{1+n}\left(a - c - \frac{b\theta}{1-t}\right) \tag{11}$$

$$T^* = \frac{n\left[b\theta - (a-c)(1-t)\right]\left[bn\theta(1-n(1-t)) - (a-c)(1-t)t\right]}{(1+n)^2(1-t)^2} \tag{12}$$

Substituting the above expressions into (6) one obtains:

$$\begin{aligned} SW^* = {} & -fn + \\ & \frac{n}{2(1+n)^2(1-t)^2}[2bc(1+n) + (a^2 + c^2 - 2fn)(2+n) + \\ & -2a(b + 2c + bn + cn)(1-t)^2 + \\ & +2b(a - b - c - cn)(1-t)\theta - b^2 n\theta^2 - 2f] \end{aligned} \tag{13}$$

Before investigating the behavior of SW^* w.r.t. θ, it is worth assessing the actual feasibility of parameters to ensure the existence of a subset of $A_{t,\theta}$ in which equilibrium outputs, profits and social welfare are all positive.

Proposition 2. *If* $f < \left(\frac{a-c}{1+n}\right)^2$, *the equilibrium profits* π_i^* *are positive for any couple of tax rates belonging to the set*

$$\begin{aligned} B_{t,\theta} := \{(t,\theta) \mid 0 < t < 1 - f[(1+n)\,/\,(a-c)]^2, \\ b^2n^2\theta^2 + b(a-c)(1+n^2)(1-t)\theta - (a-c)^2(1-t)^2 + f(1+n)^2(1-t) < 0\} \end{aligned} \tag{14}$$

Proof. Consider the expression of equilibrium profits (10). It is positive when

$$b^2n^2\theta^2 + b(a-c)(1+n^2)(1-t)\theta - (a-c)^2(1-t)^2 + f(1+n)^2(1-t) < 0, \tag{15}$$

and this inequality determines the disjoint union of two subsets of the (t,θ) plane, each one enclosed by a branch of a hyperbola with transverse axes. One of these branches intersects the t axis in $(1,0)$, which does not belong to $A_{t,\theta}$, whereas the other one crosses the horizontal axis at $t^* = 1 - f\left(\frac{1+n}{a-c}\right)^2$, which belongs to the interval $(0,1)$ if $f < \left(\frac{a-c}{1+n}\right)^2$.

This branch intersects the θ axis in two points $\theta_1 > 0$ and $\theta_2 < 0$. Then, the subset of $A_{t,\theta}$ under this arm is nonempty. In this subset, that we denote with $B_{t,\theta}$, both equilibrium outputs and profits are positive. ■

The region $B_{t,\theta}$ is portrayed in Figure 2.

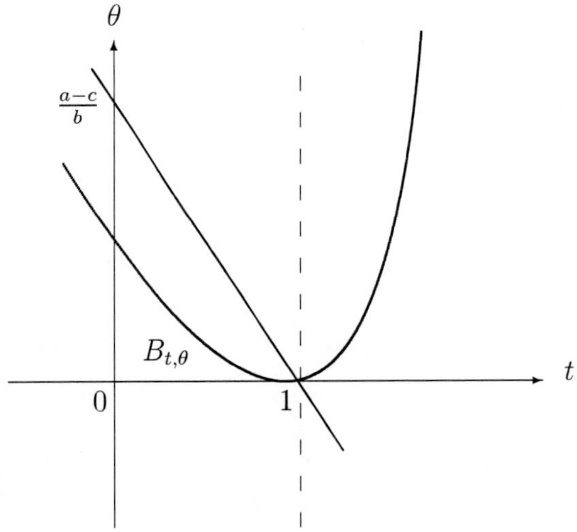

Figure 2. Region $B_{t,\theta}$.

Proposition 3. *If* $f > \dfrac{(a-c)^2}{n(1+n)^2}$ *and if*

$$b < \frac{(n-1)[-(a-c)(1+n^2)+\sqrt{(a-c)^2(1+n^4+6n^2)-4n^2f(1+n)^2}]}{2(1+n)n^2},$$

then the equilibrium social welfare SW^* is positive for any ordered pair of tax rates belonging to the set

$$C_{t,\theta} := B_{t,\theta} \cap \left\{ (t,\theta) \mid \theta > \frac{1}{bn}\left[\frac{(a-c)(1-t)t - b(1+n)(1-t)}{1-n(1-t)}\right]\right\}$$

Proof. Consider the equilibrium values (12) and (11). We have that $T^* > S^*$ if and only if

$$\frac{[b\theta-(a-c)(1-t)]\,[bn\theta(1-n(1-t))-(a-c)(1-t)t]}{(1+n)(1-t)^2} > b\left(a-c-\frac{b\theta}{1-t}\right) \tag{16}$$

Since in the set $A_{t,\theta}$ the term $a-c-\dfrac{b\theta}{1-t}$ is positive, we can divide both sides by this quantity and obtain the following inequality:

$$-[bn\theta(1-n(1-t))-(a-c)(1-t)t] > b(1+n)(1-t) \tag{17}$$

Consider now the strip $0 \leq t < 1 - \dfrac{1}{n}$ in the (t, θ) tax rate plane. In this set the previous inequality corresponds to:

$$\theta > \frac{1}{bn}\left[\frac{(a-c)(1-t)t - b(1+n)(1-t)}{1-n(1-t)}\right] \tag{18}$$

If $f > \dfrac{(a-c)^2}{n(1+n)^2}$, we have that:

$$\frac{f(1+n)^2}{(a-c)^2} > \frac{1}{n} \iff 1 - \frac{f(1+n)^2}{(a-c)^2} < 1 - \frac{1}{n}, \tag{19}$$

that is, the subset $B_{t,\theta}$ is entirely contained in the above strip. The boundary of the portion (18) is a continuous function of n such that $\theta(0) = \dfrac{n+1}{n-1} > 0$.

It follows that if this quota is lower than θ_1 and since there exists a neighborhood of 0 in which continuity holds, then there exists a subset $C_{t,\theta}$ of $B_{t,\theta}$ determined by the intersection of $B_{t,\theta}$ with (18), where $T^* > S^*$. The condition $\theta(0) < \theta_1$ can be associated to the parameter b as follows:

$$b < \frac{(n-1)[-(a-c)(1+n^2) + \sqrt{(a-c)^2(1+n^4+6n^2) - 4n^2 f(1+n)^2}]}{2(1+n)n^2} \tag{20}$$

Then, recalling (7) and (6), in the subset $C_{t,\theta}$ the related consumer surplus at equilibrium is positive and that finally entails that $SW^* > 0$ as well. ■

Region $C_{t,\theta}$ represents the region where quantities, profits and social welfare are positive. In Figure 3, it corresponds to the area below the lowest concave curve.

Now, solving $\partial SW^*/\partial\theta = 0$, one has

$$\theta^* = \frac{(1-t)\,[b\,(n+1) - a + c]}{b} > 0 \tag{21}$$

for all $b > (a-c)/(n+1)$, where the lower bound to b coincides with the optimal Cournot-Nash output in absence of any environmental policy, $q^{CN}\,(\theta = 0)$. From (21), we draw an immediate implication concerning the elasticity of substitution:

$$|\varepsilon_{\theta t}| = -\frac{\partial\theta^*}{\partial t} \cdot \frac{t}{\theta^*} = \frac{t}{1-t} \in [0, 1)\ \forall\, t \in [0, 1/2) \tag{22}$$

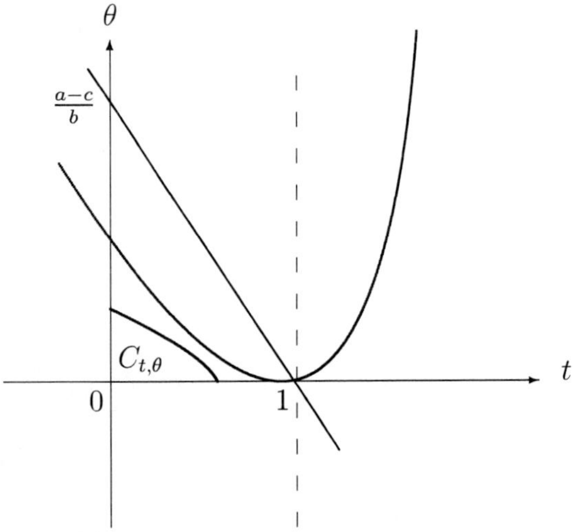

Figure 3. Region $C_{t,\theta}$.

This entails that, if different authorities manoeuvre the two tax rates, they should coordinate in order to achieve the welfare maximization that, in principle, is their common objective. In practice, the alternative between taxing and subsidizing firms in order to regulate the amount of pollution depends on parameter b. This amounts to saying that the agency in charge of the environmental policy should inform the fiscal authority about the marginal environmental impact of the technology employed by firms operating in the industry under examination.

Given the optimal environmental policy being adopted, the equilibrium output for the individual firm is

$$q_i^*(\theta^*) = \frac{a-c-b}{n} > 0 \,\forall\, b \in [0, a-c), \tag{23}$$

with $q_i^*(\theta^*) < q^{CN}(\theta = 0)$ for all $b > (a-c)/(n+1)$, entailing that, whenever firms are subject to a positive tax rate aimed at reducing the environmental externality, they restrict production as compared to the Cournot-Nash benchmark where this taxation policy is absent.

The intuitive interpretation of the above result is that, if the marginal damage from pollution is very high, then the externality effect dominates the price effect, and therefore the planner wants firms to reduce output although this involves a price increase. Exactly the opposite holds if the balance between the two effects speaks in favour of the price effect, whereby if $b < (a - c) / (n + 1)$, then θ^* indeed becomes a subsidy to firms notwithstanding the presence of the externality.

The resulting social welfare level is $SW(\theta^*) = \left[(a - c - b)^2 - 2nf\right] / 2$, which coincides with the first best level that the planner would attain by choosing directly the aggregate industry output instead of taxing polluting emissions of the n Cournot oligopolists (in this regard, see Benchekroun and Long, 1998).

5. Green R&D: Joint vs Independent Ventures

Now we will switch the focus of our analysis to include in the picture firms' incentives to carry out R&D efforts toward to attainment of green technologies. In particular, we will focus on the desirability of information transmission and the efficiency of research joint ventures vs fully non cooperative behavior when the innovation at stake is green. These issues have been discussed vigorously in the existing literature in the field, with mixed conclusions about the desirability of alternative forms of R&D cooperation (see Chiou and Hu, 2001; and Poyago-Theotoky, 2007, inter alia), the fundamental reason being that the traditional argument in favour of cooperation is a cost-saving one, which in the case under consideration may entail that any cooperation is bound to leave technology a lot more brown than one would want it to be.

To this aim, we modify the setting as follows. The industry remains a quantity-setting oligopoly but fixed entry costs can be assumed to be nil (i.e., $f = 0$), since here we abstract from the entry problem. The demand function is $p = a - Q$ and each firm produces a green R&D effort k_i, entailing a cost $\Gamma_i = zk_i^2$, $z > 0$. Each firm's emissions amount to

$$s_i = b\left(q_i - k_i - \sigma\sum_{j\neq i} k_j\right), \; i = 1, 2, ...n \tag{24}$$

which illustrates the case of an abatement technology. Parameter $\sigma \in [0, 1]$ measures the technological spillover which firm i receives from the remaining $n - 1$ firms in the industry. If $\sigma = 0$, technological spillovers are altogether absent (this being typically the case when innovation is protected by a patent system); if, instead, $\sigma = 1$, then technical knowledge is a public good, freely available to any firm in the industry as soon as any other firm has generated it (which is what happens with open innovations on the world wide web). The volume of pollution is now

$$S=\sum_{i=1}^{n}s_i=b\left(q_i-k_i-\sigma\sum_{j\neq i}k_j\right)+\sum_{j\neq i}b\left(q_j-k_j-\sigma\left(k_i+\sum_{h\neq i,j}k_h\right)\right) \tag{25}$$

Accordingly, firm i's profit function is

$$\pi_i=(p-c)\,q_i\,(1-t)-zk_i^2-\theta S \tag{26}$$

The present setting takes the form of a two-stage game, the first stage being played in the space of R&D efforts, the second in the space of output levels. To begin with, we set out under the assumption that firms play simultaneously and non cooperatively in each stage. The solution concept is the subgame perfect equilibrium by backward induction.

For the sake of simplicity, define $\alpha\equiv a-c$. The first order conditions for the Cournot-Nash equilibrium are

$$\frac{\partial\pi_i}{\partial q_i}=\left(\alpha-2q_i-\sum_{j\neq i}q_j\right)(1-t)-\theta b=0 \tag{27}$$

so that the individual output at the Cournot equilibrium is

$$q^*=\frac{\alpha\,(1-t)-b\theta}{(n+1)\,(1-t)} \tag{28}$$

Proceeding backwards to the first stage, the system of first order conditions

$$\frac{\partial\pi_i}{\partial k_i}=b\theta\,[1+\sigma\,(n-1)]-2zk_i=0 \tag{29}$$

delivers optimal symmetric R&D efforts:

$$k^*=\frac{b\theta\,[1+\sigma\,(n-1)]}{2z} \tag{30}$$

Examining the expression (30), one can quickly prove

Lemma 3. *Given $\sigma \in [0,1]$, abatement efforts are positive for all $\theta > 0$ (i.e., if the environmental policy instrument is a tax). Profit taxation has no bearings on green R&D.*

The first result appearing in the above Lemma is quite intuitive and fully aligned with the results outlined in previous research. The second claim is less obvious but it lends itself to a natural interpretation if one notes that the tax rate t only affects output decisions.

More important is the fact that, at the subgame perfect equilibrium, firms find it convenient to increase information sharing as much as possible. To verify this, it suffices to observe that expressions (28) and (30) yield the following equilibrium profits:

$$\pi^* = \frac{[\alpha(1-t) - b\theta]\left[\alpha(1-t) - n^2 b\theta\right]}{(n+1)^2(1-t)} +$$

$$\frac{b^2\theta^2\left[(n-1)^2(2n+1)\sigma^2 + 4n(n-1)\sigma + 2n - 1\right]}{4z} \tag{31}$$

which implies:

$$\frac{\partial \pi^*}{\partial \sigma} = \frac{b^2\theta^2(n-1)[2n + \sigma(n-1)(2n+1)]}{2z} > 0 \tag{32}$$

for all $n \geq 2$. The above derivative indicates that it is indeed convenient for firms to share green knowledge among themselves as much as possible, because this has the desirable consequence of diminishing the pressure exerted by Pigouvian taxation (thereby increasing profits). Moreover,

$$\frac{\partial k^*}{\partial \sigma} = \frac{b\theta(n-1)}{2z} > 0, \tag{33}$$

that is, each firm's effort is boosted by knowledge sharing. Given that this information transmission leaves outputs in expression (28) unchanged, no additional calculations are necessary to establish the following:

Proposition 4. *If green R&D takes the form of an abatement technology, then $\partial\pi^*/\partial\sigma > 0$ implies $\partial S^*/\partial\sigma < 0$.*

This amounts to saying that private (i.e., profit) incentives and collective incentives are reciprocally aligned, and information sharing is socially beneficial as it favours emission abatement. This result prompts for the analysis of a green research joint venture (RJV) in which all firms equally share the cost $\Gamma = zk^2$ of a single R&D lab in which effort k is produced, whereby the individual cost borne by firm i is $\Gamma_i = zk^2/n$ and the associated volume of polluting emissions is

$$S = b\left(q_i + \sum_{j\neq i} q_j - k\right) \tag{34}$$

What casts a shadow on the perspective of an RJV is the well known argument whereby such an organizational design of R&D activities should be resorted to in order to reduce effort duplication, which can be a sound motive for classical product or process innovations leaving aside any environmental impacts, while just the opposite can be expected to apply in the present context.

Clearly, the market stage is unmodified. At the R&D stage, every firm chooses k so as to maximize the representative firm's profit function

$$\pi^{RJV} = (\alpha - nq^*)\, q^*\,(1-t) - \frac{zk^2}{n} - \theta b\,(nq^* - k) \tag{35}$$

where q^* is defined as in (28). This procedure delivers:

$$\frac{\partial \pi^{RJV}}{\partial k} = -\frac{\partial\left(zk^2/n + \theta S\right)}{\partial k} = b\theta - \frac{2zk}{n} = 0 \Rightarrow k^{RJV} = \frac{bn\theta}{2z} \tag{36}$$

Now, on the basis of expressions (30) and (36), one can easily verify that

$$[1+\sigma(n-1)]\,k^* - \frac{k^{RJV}}{n} = \frac{b\theta\,(n-1)\,\sigma\,[2+\sigma(n-1)]}{2z} > 0 \tag{37}$$

for all $n \geq 2$ (which is obvious) and $\sigma \in [0,1)$. This exercise proves our final result:

Proposition 5. *The aggregate abatement effort is higher under fully non cooperative behavior than in a joint venture, unless technological spillovers are nil.*

The trivial corollary of the above Proposition is, clearly, that $S^{RJV} > S^*$.

Concluding Remarks

In the foregoing analysis, we have performed two tasks. First, we have studied the non-neutrality of profit taxation in an oligopoly game with negative environmental externality, concerning the effect of combined operative profit and emission tax rates on the equilibrium industry structure. Second, we have investigated the industry's incentive to perform R&D projects aimed at delivering abatement technologies under two alternative organizational settings, one being the standard independent venture with spillover effects, the other an RJV for a single lab whose costs are uniformly distributed across the entire population of firms. The second exercise has proved that (i) information sharing is both privately and socially efficient, and (ii) the fully non cooperative behavior outperforms the RJV in all cases except the one where information sharing is altogether absent.

References

[1] Benchekroun, H. and Long, N.V. (1998). Efficiency inducing taxation for polluting oligopolists. *Journal of Public Economics*, 70, 325-342.

[2] Benchekroun, H. and Long, N.V. (2002). On the multiplicity of efficiency-inducing tax rules. *Economics Letters*, 76, 331-336.

[3] Besley, T. (1989). Commodity taxation and imperfect competition: a note on the effects of entry. *Journal of Public Economics*, 40, 359-367.

[4] Bovenberg, A.L. and Goulder, L.H. (1996). Optimal environmental taxation in the presence of other taxes: general-equilibrium analyses. *American Economic Review*, 86, 985-1000.

[5] Chiou, J.-R. and Hu, J.-L. (2001). Environmental research joint ventures under emission taxes. *Environmental and Resource Economics*, 20, 129-146.

[6] Cremer, H., Ghavari, F. and Ladoux, N. (1998). Externalities and optimal taxation. *Journal of Public Economics*, 70, 343-364.

[7] Damania, D. (1996). Pollution taxes and pollution abatement in an oligopoly supergame. *Journal of Environmental Economics and Management*, 30, 323-336.

[8] Delipalla, S. and Keen, M. (1992). The comparison between ad valorem and specific taxation under imperfect competition. *Journal of Public Economics*, 49, 351-367.

[9] Denicolò, V. and Matteuzzi, M. (2000). Specific and ad valorem taxation in asymmetric Cournot oligopolies. *International Tax and Public Finance*, 7, 335-342.

[10] Dung, T.H. (1993). Optimal taxation and heterogeneous oligopoly. *Canadian Journal of Economics*, 26, 933-947.

[11] Fullerton, D. and Metcalf, G.E. (2001). Environmental controls, scarcity rents, and pre-existing distortions. *Journal of Public Economics*, 80, 249-267.

[12] Fujiwara, K. (2009). Environmental policies in a differentiated oligopoly revisited. *Resource and Energy Economics*, 31, 239-247.

[13] Goulder, L.H., Parry, I.W.H. and Burtraw, D. (1997). Revenue-raising versus other approaches to environmental protection: the critical significance of preexisting tax distortions. *RAND Journal of Economics*, 28, 708-731.

[14] Goulder, L.H., Parry, I.W.H., Williams, R.C. and Burtraw, D. (1999). The cost-effectiveness of alternative instruments for environmental protection in a second-best setting. *Journal of Public Economics*, 72, 329-360.

[15] Karp, L. and Livernois, J. (1994). Using automatic tax changes to control pollution emissions. *Journal of Environmental Economics and Management*, 27, 38-48.

[16] Katsoulacos, Y. and Xepapadeas, A. (1995). Environmental policy under oligopoly with endogenous market structure. *Scandinavian Journal of Economics*, 97, 411-420.

[17] Levin, D. (1985). Taxation within Cournot oligopoly. *Journal of Public Economics*, 27, 281-290.

[18] Mankiw, N.G. and Whinston, M.D. (1986). Free entry and social inefficiency. *RAND Journal of Economics*, 17, 48-58.

[19] Parry, I.W.H. (1997). Environmental taxes and quotas in the presence of distorting taxes in factor markets. *Resource and Energy Economics*, 19, 203-220.

[20] Parry, I.W.H. and Williams, R.C. (2001). A second-best evaluation of eight policy instruments to reduce carbon emissions. *Resource and Energy Economics*, 21, 347-373.

[21] Poyago-Theotoky, J. (2007). The organization of R&D and environmental policy. *Journal of Economic Behaviour and Organization*, 62, 63-75.

[22] Simpson, R.D. (1995). Optimal pollution taxation in a Cournot duopoly. *Environmental and Resource Economics*, 6, 359-369.

[23] Ushio, Y. (2000). Welfare effects of commodity taxation in Cournot oligopoly. *Japanese Economic Review*, 51, 268-273.

In: Economics of Environmental Policy … ISBN: 978-1-63463-165-5
Editors: M. G. Fikru and M. Insall

Chapter 3

STRATEGIC POLLUTION POLICIES: QUOTA VERSUS TAX IN INTERNATIONAL TRADE COMPETITION

Rafael Salvador Espinosa Ramirez *

Professor at the Department of Economics, Universidad de Guadalajara, Guadalajara, Mexico

ABSTRACT

In a reciprocal dumping model of trade, two groups of polluting firms, located in two countries, compete in an oligopolistic setting. We analyze the effect of the pollution quota and pollution tax imposed by the local governments on the welfare of each country. Although there is no cross border pollution, each government has to take into account the effect of setting environmental policies in both countries in order to evaluate the impact of these policies on local producers, consumer surplus and pollution disutility. We found in general that pollution policies restrict trade and reduce the producer and consumers surplus benefit. On the other hand these policies reduce harmful social pollution. In the quota case, the optimal quota will be larger with smaller harmful pollution and the efficiency of the local firms, compared with the foreign firms. In the tax case, the optimal tax will be larger with larger tax revenues and harmful pollution despite the loss in producer and consumer surplus. When the tax revenue and the harmful pollution are small, the

* Corresponding author: E-mail: rafaelsa@cucea.udg.mx.

government is willing to set a subsidy in order to encourage the consumer and producer surplus. Both policies coincide in the case in which the marginal disutility is very high and the negative effect of pollution is larger than the other components of the welfare function. On the other hand, when the marginal disutility is relatively small, the policies in both cases are different. In the case of quota, the optimal policy depends on their relationship with the magnitude of the abatement pollution cost. In the case of a tax, the optimal policies depend on the number of firms existing in each country. The model emphasizes the importance of establishing strategic rational environmental policies in order to maximize the competitiveness of firms, the expected benefits for consumers, and to minimize the impact of harmful pollution.

1. Introduction

Greenhouse effect, acid rain, additives and the change in the temperature of the oceans are only a few adverse consequences caused by pollution. According to the Intergovernmental Panel on Climate Change (IPCC) in its 2007 report, one of the main causes of Global Warming is given by the anthropogenic factors. Specifically speaking 90% of the greenhouse gases, which are the main cause of Global Warming, are produced by human activities in the form of pollution. It is stated in the IPCC (2007) report that Global Warming is the cause of most natural disasters. Therefore, pollution is to blame for the increase in the social and economic costs caused by natural disasters like hurricanes, twisters and floods. According to the Extreme Weather Sourcebook 2008 (National Center for Atmospheric Research, US) hurricanes, twisters and floods have cost the US government a yearly average of 16,972,000 U.S. Dollars in the 1955-2006 period. In some years the cost reached more than 100 billion U.S. Dollars. Moreover, the effect of pollution on the health of people has reached alarming levels. Due to pollution, respiratory illnesses have increased 200%, intestinal illnesses 110%, and additional illnesses 75% in the last ten years according to the 2007 Report of the World Health Organization.

These devastating effects of pollution in the world call for a coordinated effort made by the governments all over the world. An example of this attempt was the unsuccessful Rio Conference in Brazil 1992, and the 2002 Johannesburg Summit. The intensive use of natural resources and intensity production process is blamed as the main cause of pollution. However, the governments are not willing to apply policies to reduce pollution since these policies may increase the industrial costs and undermine the international competitiveness of domestic industries. In this sense, pollution control is a barrier to trade and, nowadays, it is extensively discussed in the free trade agreements.

Even though there is a vast literature on environmental regulations as presented by Cropper and Oates (1992), the existing literature on environmental regulations and trade competition has not been sufficiently explored. This is our main motivation in this chapter as we try to analyze the welfare effects of pollution regulation when trade takes place between two similar countries in the presence of production competition.

We consider two types of policies: pollution tax and pollution quota. This chapter will discuss the impact of each policy on welfare of the government, since the environment policy implemented may be different according to the specific environmental objectives. One example is the discussion between carbon tax and cap-and-trade system (quotas). There is much discussion about whether a carbon tax or a cap-and-trade system is the best way to put a price on greenhouse gas pollution. The answer depends on how each system is designed. The design will determine the environmental and economic effectiveness. Sweden has used a carbon tax to reduce greenhouse gas emissions since 1991. Canada B. C. and Quebec use carbon taxes as part of their strategies to reduce emissions and encourage investments in energy-efficiency and renewable energy. In the case of quotas, cap-and-trade has been used successfully in the U.S. to reduce emissions of sulphur dioxide and nitrous oxide, and the European Union has had a cap-and-trade system in place since 2005 to reduce greenhouse gas emissions from about 10,000 large industrial emitters.

On the other hand, trade between similar products, such as the reciprocal export of coffee between Mexico and Costa Rica, is an assumption that we will consider on this chapter. The natural explanation is that Costa Rica coffee is slightly different from Mexican coffee, so some consumers in each market prefer foreign coffee. This two-way trade in similar (but not strictly identical) products is called intra-industry trade.[1] It has also been referred to as cross-hauling and has been discussed in the point-pricing literature of perfect competition. However, many attempts have been made at imperfect competitive framework and especially in a Cournot oligopolistic setting like in Brander (1981) and Brander and Krugman (1983).

---

[1] Seminal papers on intra-industry trade are Balassa (1966), Krugman (1979) and Lancaster (1980).

Brander and Krugman (1983) prove that the rivalry of oligopolistic firms serves as an independent cause of international trade. Such rivalry naturally gives rise to 'dumping' of output in foreign markets. Such dumping can be 'reciprocal', that is, there may be a two-way trade in the same product and it can be explained by the standard theory of monopolistic price discrimination.[2] On the other hand, they also show that reciprocal dumping is rather striking in that there is pure waste in the form of unnecessary transport costs. Without free entry and low transport costs, welfare may improve as trade opens up and reciprocal dumping occurs. But it is also possible that welfare may decline with high transport costs.

In the present chapter we assume that firms located within a country have the same marginal costs, but different from those firms located in the other country. We also assume that there is environmental degradation as a result of the production process. In a reciprocal dumping model we analyze the setting of pollution quota and pollution tax restriction to determine the effect of the environmental policies on the welfare of each country. Although there is no cross border pollution, each country must take into account the effect of environmental policies (local and foreign) on the producer surplus, consumer surplus and pollution disutility on local welfare.

The model is spelled out in detail in the following section. In Subsections *3* we derive (in a non-cooperative equilibrium) the properties of the optimal pollution quota and tax respectively. Section *4* analyzes the two policy regimes. Finally, some concluding remarks are made in section *5*.

2. THE MODEL

We assume that there are two countries having a two way trade; country A and country B. There are a certain number of firms in both countries. All firms in both countries produce the same homogeneous good and some amount of pollution arises in the production process. In this sense we assume there is a negative externality caused by this pollution.

We consider a partial equilibrium model of an oligopolistic industry in which there are n identical firms in A, and m identical firms in B such that n and m take an integer value where $n \geq 1$ and $m \geq 1$. Each firm has a Cournot perception: each firm takes the output of other firms as a given while maximizing its products.

[2] A good survey is provided by Caves and Jones (1977).

All firms in country A are identical, and all firms in country B are identical. Cost structure among n firms and among m firms are symmetrical with respect to their own type. Therefore, we can assume that the output produced by each firm in A and B is the same with respect to their own type. The marginal costs of each firm inside country A and country B are K_r and K_s respectively. In here, and for the remaining of the chapter, r and s are the notations for the firms (their components and policies) located in country A and country B respectively.

These marginal costs are taken to be constant, and therefore equal the average variable costs.[3] A part of K_j ($j = r, s$) is given by technology and factor market conditions, and another part is policy induced, and this will be spelled out later on. There is an identical transport cost t incurred in exporting goods from one country to the other, which is borne by the producers.

The homogeneous output produced by each firm located in A and B are X_A and X_B respectively. It means that X_A and X_B are the quantities of same good but produced in different countries. In here $X_A = X_A^A + X_A^B$ and $X_B = X_B^A + X_B^B$, where the subscripts indicate which country produces and the superscripts indicate which country consumes. So, X_A^A is produced and consumed in country A and X_A^B is produced in country A and exported to country B. Similarly, X_B^B is produced and consumed in country B and X_B^A is produced in country B and exported to country A.

We have segmented markets with homogeneous goods, and the inverse demand functions are: [4]

$$P_A = a - bD_A \tag{1}$$

$$P_B = a - bD_B \tag{2}$$

where

$$D_A = nX_A^A + mX_B^A \tag{3}$$

$$D_B = nX_A^B + mX_B^B \tag{4}$$

[3] Implicitly, there is a numeraire good in the background, which is produced under competitive conditions. There is also just one factor of production in each country whose price is determined in the competitive sector.

[4] We assume that the utility functions, in each country, can be approximated by $U_A = u(X_A^A, X_B^A) + \mu_A$ and $U_B = u(X_A^B, X_B^B) + \mu_B$ where X and Y are the goods under consideration and μ_A and μ_B are the expenditures on the numeraire goods. The use of this approximation removes a number of theoretical difficulties, including income effects. For simplicity, we consider identical preferences and therefore the demand parameters are identical in both countries.

The profits of each firm located in *A* and *B* are given by

$$\Pi_A = (P_A - K_r)X_A^A + (P_B - K_r - t)X_A^B \tag{5}$$

$$\Pi_B = (P_B - K_s)X_B^B + (P_A - K_s - t)X_B^A \tag{6}$$

Each firm decides how much production is for domestic consumption and how much is for exporting. Under Cournot-Nash assumptions the first order maximization conditions are:

$$a - K_r = b(n+1)X_A^A - bmX_B^A \tag{7}$$

$$a - K_r - t = b(n+1)X_A^B - bmX_B^B \tag{8}$$

$$a - K_s = b(m+1)X_B^B - bnX_A^B \tag{9}$$

$$a - K_s - t = b(m+1)X_B^A - bnX_A^A \tag{10}$$

such that we have a separable system given by the assumption of constant marginal costs. Equation (7) and (10) are solved for the market in country *A*, and equations (8) and (9) are solved for the market in country *B*. Positive solutions to this system give us the equilibrium where two-way trade arises and, given the linearity of demand functions, the second order conditions are satisfied. The closed solution forms are

$$\Pi_\mathrm{A} = b(X_A^A)^2 + b(X_A^B)^2 \tag{11}$$

$$\Pi_\mathrm{A} = b(X_B^B)^2 + b(X_B^A)^2 \tag{12}$$

$$X_B^A = \frac{(n+1)(a-K_s-t)-n(a-K_r)}{b(m+n+1)} \tag{13}$$

$$X_A^A = \frac{(m+1)(a-K_r)-m(a-K_s-t)}{b(m+n+1)} \tag{14}$$

$$X_A^B = \frac{(m+1)(a-K_r-t)-m(a-K_s)}{b(m+n+1)} \tag{15}$$

$$X_B^B = \frac{(n+1)(a-K_s)-n(a-K_r-t)}{b(m+n+1)} \tag{16}$$

The equations (1) - (6) and (11)-(16) form the backbone for the following analysis.

Once we have set the closed solution forms, we will set the welfare of each country taking into account the use of pollution quota or pollution tax. The welfare of each country, W_i $(i = A, B)$ can be written as,

$$W_A = n\Pi_A + CS_A + \Omega_A \tag{17}$$

$$W_B = m\Pi_B + CS_B + \Omega_B \tag{18}$$

where

$\Omega_i = -\psi_i Z_i$ is for the pollution quota policy case or,
$\Omega_i = \tau_j Z_i - \psi_i Z_i$ is for the pollution tax policy case.

In (17) and (18) $n\Pi_A$ y $m\Pi_B$ are the producer surplus of firms located in *A* and *B* respectively. CS_i is the consumer surplus and it is well known that

$$CS_A = bD_A^2/2 \tag{19}$$

$$CS_B = bD_B^2/2 \tag{20}$$

Ω_i is the pollution-policy impact on welfare given by the government induced policy. In the case of a pollution quota, the impact on welfare will be given by $(\Omega_i = -\psi_i Z_i)$. On the other hand, in the case of pollution tax, the impact on welfare will be given by $(\Omega_i = \tau_j Z_i - \psi_i Z_i)$. As mentioned before since we are considering a small economy, we ignore cross-border pollution.

In both cases Z_i is the total amount of harmful pollution in country i. It is the gross emission or total release of pollutants to air, water or land (e.g. ton sulphur dioxide and nitrous oxide); and the source of negative externality. Z_i is defined as $Z_A = nz_r X_A$ and $Z_B = mz_s X_B$ for country *A* and *B* respectively. z_j $(j = r, s)$ is the amount of pollution per unit of output produced by each firm in each country, which is the same for all firms in *A* and is the same for all firms in *B* (e.g. ton sulphur dioxide and nitrous oxide per output by each firm). If the firms were non-polluting, Z_i would be zero. ψ_i is the marginal disutility of pollution which we assume, as do Lahiri and Ono (1998) and Markusen, *et.*

al. (1993 and 1995), is constant.[5] In order to keep the analysis at a tractable level, we assume that the marginal disutility of pollution in both countries is the same. Apart from some particular exceptions, the damage of pollution on any human being is generally identical so that $\psi_A = \psi_B = \psi$.

In the case of pollution quota, the government is going to determine the level of allowed pollution emitted by firms per unit of output (z_j), and consequently the amount of disutility for pollution. On the other hand, in the case of a pollution tax, we should consider the negative impact of pollution disutility plus the term called tax revenue ($\tau_j Z_i$). In here the government is not going to determine the amount of pollution produced per unit of output, but the optimal pollution tax (τ_j). This is a per-unit tax levied to each firm; it is the tax per unit of z_j produced. In the next section we are going to determine both the optimal pollution tax and pollution quota policies.

3. Optimal Polices

In this section, we will determine the optimal pollution policies. Pollution quota and pollution tax are the most common formal policies used to obtain some control on pollution emissions. The impact of both policies on welfare may be rather different. In the next subsections we will analyze pollution quota and pollution tax taking into account the welfare maximizing option.

3.1. Pollution Quota

The first policy to analyze is the pollution quota. This policy is a restriction on the amount of pollution that is allowed to each firm as a result of the production process. In order to do the analysis, we define K_j (as seen in (5) and (6)) as follows;

$$K_j = C_j + T_j \tag{21}$$

where C_j is the part of the unit cost in each firm that is determined by technological and factor market conditions (it will be called simply marginal

[5] Other authors, like Asako (1979), consider that marginal disutility is an increasing function of the output. However, this alternative assumption will not contradict our results and a constant marginal disutility is a more convenient assumption.

cost), and is taken to be constant. As the production of X_A and X_B implies emission of pollution, T_j is the unit policy-induced cost of pollution abatement in each firm. This policy-induced cost is defined like in Lahiri and Ono (1998) as

$$T_j = \gamma(\theta - z_j) \tag{22}$$

where for simplicity θ and γ are the same in both countries. θ is the amount of pollution per-unit of output produced so that θX_A and θX_B are the total amount of pollution produced per firm (before any abatement) located in country A and B respectively.[6] z_j is the maximum quantity of pollution per unit of output produced that each firm in country i is allowed to emit into the atmosphere.[7] While θ is what each firm would regularly emit per unit of output (because of their technology, etc.), z_j is what the government requires as a maximum allowable pollution per output, and θ minus z_j is what the firm ends up cleaning due to the policy. The case in which $\theta < z_j$ is not going to be considered because it means the government is willing to encourage pollution far from the technical limits. Even when it is possible, this policy seems politically incorrect and it is not the case for this chapter.

We assume that the abatement technology is such that it costs each firm a constant amount γ to abate one unit of pollution per unit output produced and it is identical in both countries. The parameters γ and θ together with the policy instrument used by the government will determine the policy-induced part of the unit cost K_j's.

From total differentiation of demands (13)-(16) and (21)-(22) we have:

$$dX_A^A = dX_A^B = \frac{(m+1)\gamma}{b\alpha} dz_r - \frac{m\gamma}{b\alpha} dz_s \tag{23}$$

$$dX_B^A = dX_B^B = \frac{(n+1)\gamma}{b\alpha} dz_s - \frac{n\gamma}{b\alpha} dz_r \tag{24}$$

where $\alpha = m + n + 1$.

6 Implicitly, this unit pollution parameter is taken to be over and above the level, which the World Health Organization (WHO) considers to be harmless. On the other hand, $n\theta X$ and $m\theta Y$ are the countries' total pollution produced by A and B respectively before any abatement.

7 Like in the case of θ, these instruments are taken to be over and above the level, which the WHO considers to be harmless.

From (11)-(16), (19), (20), (23) and (24), we obtain the total differentiation of (17) and (18) with respect to the pollution quota policies in the following expressions:

$$dW_A = \frac{n}{b\alpha}[bD_A\gamma + 2b(m+1)\gamma X_A - b\alpha X_A\psi - z_r 2(m+1)\Upsilon\psi]dz_r + \frac{m}{b\alpha}[bD_A\gamma - 2n\gamma bX_A + z_r 2n\gamma]dz_s \tag{25}$$

$$dW_B = \frac{m}{b\alpha}[bD_B\gamma + 2b(n+1)\gamma X_B - b\alpha X_B\psi - z_s 2(n+1)\Upsilon\psi]dz_s + \frac{n}{b\alpha}[bD_B\gamma - 2m\gamma bX_B + z_s 2m\gamma]dz_r \tag{26}$$

In here we have two square brackets in each equation (25) and (26). The first square bracket in (25) and (26) shows the effect of the local policy on local welfare and the second square bracket in (25) and (26) shows the effect of the foreign policy on local welfare. The first term inside the square brackets in (25) and (26) is the consumers' surplus effect. It is unambiguously positive to any pollution quota and positive outputs in both countries. An increase in the allowed pollution quota (local or foreign) will reduce the cost for abatement pollution of the firms and consequently will increase the amount of output produced, reducing the price for consumers.

The second term inside the square brackets in (25) and (26) is the producer surplus effect. With an increase in the allowed local pollution quota, the cost for local firms will be reduced and their producer surplus will increase. The local firms will have a competitive advantage over the foreign competitors and the producer surplus of the foreign firms will be reduced.

Finally, the remaining terms inside the square brackets in (25) y (26) represent the harmful pollution effect. When more pollution is allowed in a local country, the local welfare will then be reduced by a larger negative impact on the people's health. There is an increase in quota, production and thus in harmful pollution. On the other hand, when the foreign country allows a higher pollution quota, the cost of foreign firms will decrease. So, the local firms become less competitive and the local production and harmful local pollution will be reduced. There will be a benefit on the health of local people.

Taking into account the assumptions made before, for the welfare functions to be concave in z_r and z_s, we must have

$$\frac{d^2W_A}{dz_r^2} = \frac{n\gamma}{b\alpha^2}[(\gamma - \psi)(4(m+1)^2) + 4n(\gamma - (m+1)\psi)] < 0$$

$$\frac{d^2W_B}{dz_s^2} = \frac{m\gamma}{b\alpha^2}[(\gamma - \psi)(4(n+1)^2) + 4m(\gamma - (n+1)\psi)] < 0$$

Clearly the above conditions are satisfied if

$$\psi > \gamma\Delta_A$$

$$\psi > \gamma\Delta_B$$

where

$$\Delta_A = \frac{(m+1)m+\alpha}{(m+1)\alpha} < 1$$

$$\Delta_B = \frac{(n+1)n+\alpha}{(n+1)\alpha} < 1$$

These conditions imply the existence of a minimum level of marginal damage for the result to hold. How large should the marginal disutility be? There is not a specific level of marginal damage. The marginal disutility could be larger or smaller than the marginal cost for abating pollution, and it is going to depend on the number of competing firms. The only certain claim is that the marginal damage must be positive. We will consider only the cases in which the second order conditions hold with feasible outputs.

We consider the case where the governments behave in a non-cooperative fashion to obtain the non-cooperative Nash pollution levels of emission standards, z_r^N and z_s^N. Setting the coefficients of dz_r and dz_s from (25) and (26) respectively equal to zero we get

$$z_r^N = \frac{b}{\gamma\psi 2(m+1)}[(2\gamma - \psi)\alpha X_A + \gamma(mX_B^A - nX_A^B)] \tag{27}$$

$$z_s^N = \frac{b}{\gamma\psi 2(n+1)}[(2\gamma - \psi)\alpha X_B + \gamma(nX_A^B - mX_B^A)] \tag{28}$$

The optimal values of z_A^N and z_B^N have been not yet been fully characterized. Apart from the marginal costs of C_r and C_s (expressed in X_A and X_B differences), other parameters affecting the values of z_r^N and z_s^N are the marginal disutility level ψ and the marginal cost of abatement pollution γ. When γ is very small, imposing pollution control has no costs but only benefits. Therefore the optimal policy in both countries is to impose the most severe pollution restrictions, i.e. $z_r^N = 0$ and $z_s^N = 0$. On the other hand, when

γ is greater than or equal to ψ both policy instruments are positive. Formally we can write the following proposition

Proposition 1. *In a reciprocal dumping model of trade, at the non-cooperative equilibrium, the optimal pollution quotas are given by the followings:*

1. $if\ \psi \gg \gamma, then\ z_r^N = z_s^N = 0$
2. $if\ \gamma \geq \psi, then\ z_r^N > 0, z_s^N > 0$
3. $if\ \psi \simeq 2\gamma$
   a. $and\ C_r \gg C_s, then\ z_r^N > 0, z_s^N = 0$
   b. $and\ C_r \ll C_s, then\ z_r^N = 0, z_s^N > 0$

This proposition can be explained intuitively as follows. When the marginal disutility for pollution is sufficiently bigger than the marginal cost for abating pollution ($\psi \gg \gamma$), the harmful effect of pollution outweighs the benefit obtained by the producer and consumer surplus. The government sets the severest pollution policy as it reduces the optimal output and consequently the pollution level.

On the other hand, a larger or equal marginal cost of abatement pollution than marginal disutility for pollution ($\gamma \geq \psi$) means that pollution control has a negative impact on production and price. A reduction in output reduces the producer surplus, increases the prices and reduces the consumers' surplus. Therefore, in this case ($\gamma \geq \psi$), the government is forced to allow a positive amount of pollution.

As a third result, we have the case in which the difference between ψ and γ is no longer decisive ($\psi \simeq 2\gamma$). If there is a large difference between marginal costs (C_r, C_s), the more inefficient country will be lax in the restrictions on pollution whilst the efficient country will apply the severest restrictions. In the inefficient country the output will be small and the government will have incentives to increase the production reducing the industrial cost through a positive quota. In the efficient country the output, and consequently the pollution, will be larger. In this country the pollution disutility will be greater than the producer surplus and consumer surplus, and the government will apply the severest pollution quota. [8]

[8] With a monopoly in each country ($m = n = 1$), this result can be seen from the difference between optimal polices as in Espinosa (2008) where

3.2. Pollution Tax

Once we have set the optimal pollution quota, we shall analyze in this section the optimal pollution tax as another common policy used to control pollution degradation. First of all, the cost structure in the case of pollution tax is different than that of pollution quota. Even when the unit cost determined by the technological and factor market conditions is the same, the policy induced cost T_j is defined as

$$T_j = \gamma(\theta - z_j) + \tau_j z_j \tag{29}$$

where the first term in (29) is similar to the pollution quota case.

However, in (29), z_r and z_s are different because they are not determined by the government but by the firms. They represent the amount of emitted pollution that agents impose themselves in order to reduce the cost. So, z_j is the maximum quantity of pollution per unit of output that the firms in country i allowed themselves to emit into the atmosphere. There is a self-restriction and we assume that the firms possess the proper technology to abate such pollution. This self-restriction is going to depend on the magnitude of the tax levied by the government.

On the other hand, $\tau_j z_j$ in (29) is the tax revenue, which is the amount of income received by the government after levying a tax on each polluting firm. The government is going to set the optimal tax in order to maximize the social welfare.

We can see from (29) that the policy-induced cost has two components: the firms allow themselves to produce pollution but they have to pay a tax to do so, and besides, they have a cost to fight against the pollution not allowed. In this sense, the firms are going to decide the level of allowed pollution taking into account the level of tax levied by the government. From (29) we can get:

$$z_j = \begin{cases} 0 & \text{if } \tau_j \geq \gamma \\ \theta & \text{if } \tau_j < \gamma \end{cases} \tag{30}$$

$$z_r^N - z_s^N = \frac{2\gamma + 3\psi}{5\psi\gamma}(C_r - C_s)$$

The more inefficient country will allow a greater amount of pollution per-unit of output.

If the tax is larger than the cost of abatement pollution, producing pollution will be costly and the best option is not to allow pollution at all. It is cheaper to abate all pollution than pay tax for it. On the other hand, if the tax is smaller than the cost of abatement pollution, then abating pollution is clearly costly and the firms are willing to allow all the possible pollution and pay a tax for it. In the case in which the tax is equal to the cost of abatement pollution, the firms would be indifferent between allowing all the pollution or do not pollute at all. However, for simplicity, we will consider that in this case the firms will abate all pollution. The marginal cost of the firms (from (21) and (30)) can be written as

$$\mathrm{K_j} = \begin{cases} C_j + \gamma\theta & \text{if } \tau_j \geq \gamma \\ C_j + \tau_j\theta & \text{if } \tau_j < \gamma \end{cases} \tag{31}$$

In order to get the optimal tax we have to consider only the case in which the tax is smaller than the cost of abatement ($\tau_j < \gamma$). The case in which ($\tau_j \geq \gamma$), there is no pollution produced and therefore the impact of tax on welfare is null. The calculus of the optimal tax, under this last condition, does not make sense and therefore we will only consider the case in which the optimal tax is smaller than the abatement cost. Therefore from (30) we have $z_j = \theta$. Taking total differentiation of demands (13)-(16) and (21) and (30) we get:

$$dX_A^A = dX_A^B = -\frac{\theta(m+1)}{b\alpha} d\tau_r + \frac{\theta m}{b\alpha} d\tau_s \tag{32}$$

$$dX_B^A = dX_B^B = \frac{\theta n}{b\alpha} d\tau_r - \frac{\theta(n+1)}{b\alpha} d\tau_s \tag{33}$$

From (11)-(16), (19), (20), (32) and (33), we obtain the total differentiation of (17) and (18) with respect to the pollution tax policies in the following expressions:

$$dW_A = \left[-\frac{nD_A\theta}{\alpha} - \frac{2X_A\theta(m+1)n}{\alpha} + n\theta X_A + (\psi - \tau_r)\left(\frac{n2\theta^2(m+1)}{b\alpha}\right)\right] d\tau_r + \left[-\frac{mD_A\theta}{\alpha} + \frac{2\theta mnX_A}{\alpha} - (\psi - \tau_r)\left(\frac{n2\theta^2 m}{b\alpha}\right)\right] d\tau_s \tag{34}$$

$$dW_B = \left[-\frac{mD_B\theta}{\alpha} - \frac{2\theta m(n+1)X_B}{\alpha} + m\theta X_B + (\psi - \tau_s)\left(\frac{m2\theta^2(n+1)}{b\alpha}\right)\right] d\tau_s + \left[-\frac{nD_B\theta}{\alpha} + \frac{2\theta mnX_B}{\alpha} - (\psi - \tau_s)\left(\frac{n2\theta^2 m}{b\alpha}\right)\right] d\tau_r \tag{35}$$

As in the quota case, in here we have two square brackets in each equation (34) and (35). The first square bracket in (34) and (35) shows the effect of the local policy on local welfare and the second square bracket in (34) and (35) shows the effect of the foreign policy on local welfare.

The first term inside the square brackets in (34) and (35) is the consumer surplus effect of a pollution tax on welfare, which is negative. Clearly, an increase in tax will increase the production cost. This higher cost will reduce the output and consequently will increase the price for the consumers.

The second term inside the square brackets in (34) and (35) is the producer surplus effect, which is ambiguous. When the government in a local country increases the pollution tax to the local producer, there is an increase in the production cost. The higher cost gives to local firms a competitive disadvantage over the foreign firms. The output of domestic firms will be reduced and the output of foreign firms will increase. The local producer surplus will decrease and the foreign producer surplus will increase.

The remaining terms inside the square brackets in (34) and (35) are the pollution policy impact on welfare. In the case of pollution tax, the pollution policy impact on welfare has two components: the harm of pollution on the welfare of the government and the tax revenue. As we have seen before, an increase in the local pollution tax will reduce the output of the local firms and will increase the output of foreign firms. In this sense, an increase in local tax will reduce the amount of harmful pollution produced by local firms. However, the harmful pollution in the foreign country will increase as the output of foreign firms will increase as well.

In the case of tax revenue, there is a direct and an indirect effect of increasing a tax. There is a direct positive effect given by the increase in the tax itself. On the other hand, the indirect effect comes from the reduction in the local output and consequently in the amount of taxes collected. In other words the effect of an increase on tax is ambiguous and is going to depend on the magnitude of the direct and indirect effects.

Taking into account the concavity of the welfare functions and the assumption of feasible output, we consider again the case in which the government behaves in a non-cooperative fashion to obtain the optimal pollution tax[9]. Setting the coefficients of $d\tau_r$ and $d\tau_s$ from (34) and (35) respectively equal to zero we get:

$$\tau_r = -\frac{b}{2(m+1)\theta}[mX_B^A + (m+1)X_A^A + X_A^B(m+1-n)] + \psi \tag{36}$$

$$\tau_s = -\frac{b}{2(n+1)\theta}[nX_A^B + (n+1)X_B^B + X_B^A(n+1-m)] + \psi \tag{37}$$

The results are pretty ambiguous. In (36) and (37) we can find two parameters determining the value of the taxes: the marginal disutility of pollution and the proportion of local and foreign firms production.

First of all, let´s assume that the cost structure given by technological and factor market conditions are similar between countries ($C_s \sim C_r$) such that $X_A^B \sim X_B^A$. We assume a small transport cost as well. When the marginal disutility of pollution is sufficiently small ($\psi \simeq 0$), then the optimal taxes would depend on the number of firms located in each country. With a sufficiently large difference between the number of firms located in each country, the country with the larger number of firms will set the most severe pollution policy and the country with the least number of firms will set a subsidy. With the same number of firms between countries, both governments will set a subsidy. On the other hand, with a large pollution impact ($\psi \gg 0$), both governments will set a severe pollution policy in order to reduce the negative impact of pollution on the health of the people.

It is naive to say that a large difference in cost structure between countries is a source of more ambiguity. Formally we can set:

Proposition 2. *In a reciprocal dumping model of trade, at the non-cooperative equilibrium, the optimal pollution taxes are given by the following:*

1. If $\psi \simeq 0$ *and* $\begin{cases} n \gg m \; then \; \tau_r > 0 \; and \; \tau_s < 0 \\ n \ll m \; then \; \tau_r < 0 \; and \; \tau_s > 0 \\ n \approx m \; then \; \tau_r < 0 \; and \; \tau_s < 0 \end{cases}$
2. If $\psi \gg 0 \; then \; \tau_r > 0 \; and \; \tau_s > 0$

[9] Obtaining the second derivative from the welfare function we get

$$\frac{d^2W_A}{d\tau_r^2} = -\frac{n^2\theta^2(4m+3)}{b\alpha} < 0 \text{ and } \frac{d^2W_B}{d\tau_s^2} = -\frac{m^2\theta^2(4n+3)}{b\alpha} < 0.$$

Intuitively speaking, the optimal tax is a decision in which the governments are weighting the consumer and producer surplus on one hand, and the tax revenue and the harmful pollution on the other.

When the effect of pollution on the health of the people is negligible in both countries, the tax set is going to depend on the number of domestic and foreign firms. When the number of firms domestically located is sufficiently larger than the foreign firms, the tax revenue outweighs the benefit in consumer and producer surplus. So the domestic government is willing to set a positive tax in order to benefit from the large tax revenue despite the loss in consumer and producer surplus. On the other hand, the foreign country is willing to set a subsidy in order to benefit from the competitive advantage of their firms and gain from producer and consumer surplus. When countries have the same number of firms, there is no competitive advantage and both countries will set a subsidy in order to benefit from the consumer and producer surplus despite the loss in tax revenue.

In a second case, when the effect of pollution on the health of the people is sufficiently large in both countries, the governments have incentives to set a positive tax in order to reduce the impact of pollution on people's health. It is always possible to have a high level of pollution damage to pursue a strict environmental policy. The pollution disutility emphasizes the government's willingness to set a pollution tax in order to reduce the harmful pollution.

4. Policy Comparison

Probably the most interesting feature of the reciprocal dumping analysis is the policy strategies used in the context of segmented markets. The optimal policy should take into account not only the impact on the local market but also on the foreign market and the benefit obtained through producer and consumer surplus. Even when a local policy may bring some direct effects on local welfare by affecting local market conditions, the foreign market changes may significantly impact local welfare as well.

The use of certain policies in the context of reciprocal dumping may affect not only the market conditions, but also the competitive features. Quotas and taxes are different not only because of the tax revenue of the latter, but also by the conditions under which the competition among firms operate. The policy strategy set by a government may be different according to the condition in which the policy is implemented, and may be different even between countries.

In the case of quotas, where there is no fiscal benefit by collecting taxes, the policy decision is mainly ruled by the environmental impact on the health of the people. With the assumption of identical marginal disutility in both countries, the optimal quota generally has the same sense in both countries according to the model developed above.

In the case in which we have a marginal disutility of pollution, relatively larger than the pollution cost for abating pollution ($\psi \gg \gamma$), the cost for abating pollution is perceived as negligible and the firms are encouraged to produce more, and consequently they emit more pollution into the atmosphere. As the pollution disutility is large, the governments in both countries are willing to impose the severest policy restriction. On the other hand, when the marginal disutility of pollution is equal or smaller than the marginal cost for abating pollution, both governments set a policy addressed to allow pollution in order to benefit from consumer and producer surplus. In this case there is no significant impact on the health of the people by pollution.

If the quota determines the allowed amount of pollution per unit of output emitted into the atmosphere, in the case of taxes the firms are free to allow pollution. The existence of taxes addresses the control of polluting emissions by controlling the output produced rather than directly controlling the amount of pollution per unit of output.

Contrary to quotas, in the case of taxes there exist competitive differences determining different optimal policies between countries. The number of firms in the countries not only determines the amount of tax revenue (which is not necessarily linked between countries), but also the competitive conditions inside and outside the country where the policy is set. So the policies are linked by competition conditions between firms and countries.

When the number of firms in the local country is larger than the number of firms on the foreign country, the tax collected by the local government is an important decision variable. The amount of income received by levying a tax drives to reduce the amount of pollution emitted into the atmosphere by restricting the output produced. The local government is going to set a severe pollution policy independently of the marginal disutility of pollution. Different than the quota, in the case of tax, the most severe policy may be set even with a small marginal pollution disutility. The tax revenue collected by the local government is the main reason for this result. Additionally, in the case where we have a large marginal disutility of pollution, the willingness of setting a severe pollution tax reinforces the incentive to lessen the impact of pollution on the health of the people.

However, taking into account that the number of firms in the local country is larger than the number of firms in the foreign country, as mentioned above, the tax revenue collected by the foreign government is negligible. The foreign firms face less competition and they get some monopolistic advantage in the producer and consumer surpluses. With a negligible pollution impact on the health of the people, the foreign government is going to set a subsidy promoting production as in the quota case. On the other hand, with a sufficiently large marginal pollution disutility, the foreign government sets a tax independent of the loss in consumer and producer surpluses.

Finally, when the number of firms is the same between countries and we have a small marginal pollution disutility, both countries will set a tax pollution policy: the results are the same in the quota and tax cases. In the case of a large marginal pollution disutility the impact on health is important and both countries will set the severest pollution policy.

CONCLUSION

Nations recognize that creation, implementation and business survival are essential activities for their economic progress. However, they must take into account, in a conscientious way, the environmental implications of these activities. Thus, a detailed analysis of such implications is crucial to set the applicable regulatory policies that maximize the welfare of businesses and consumers, preserving the environmental targets at the same time.

In this context, governments are reluctant to establish firm controls for environmental protection as these policies involve increasing production costs. Pollution control undermines the competitiveness and discourages creation and survival of domestic firms, as well as the attraction of foreign investment.

In this sense environmental regulations are considered as trade barriers. These regulations are vigorously debated in international forums and on negotiations of free trade agreements. Particularly, these negotiations should take into account how the pollution regulations affect developing and developed economies in different ways. Developing economies are much more concerned about environmental regulations as they have significant exposure to the establishment of polluting firms on their territories. On the other hand, industrial activity is one of the most important activities for development, so these countries and their governments must consider both their economic interests and the preservation of natural resources and the cleanliness of their environment in the short, medium and long term.

We develop a model of Cournot oligopoly, of partial equilibrium under conditions of reciprocal dumping between two countries. We consider the domestic and foreign firms' production for local consumption and for export. Firms generate pollution in their production processes, but in turn, they have the appropriate technology to bring it down. We use two of the most used environmental policy instruments to carry on our analysis: quotas (quantitative limits on the emission of pollutants) and taxes (amount charged per unit of pollution emitted).

Concerning quotas, we calculate the optimal quota of pollution that maximizes the welfare in each country. In addition, such quantities determine the optimal strategic policy followed by each country in which each government considers the relations between the cost structure of firms, particularly the amount of the abatement cost per unit of pollution, and the marginal pollution disutility. Such policies have important involvement on the social welfare function in both countries. These welfare functions include the consumer surplus, the firm benefits and the social cost for pollution.

With quotas, there are three important cases. In the first case, if the cost of abatement is sufficiently smaller than the large marginal disutility of pollution, the optimal policy will be to impose the most restrictive quota. In this case the government gives priority to protecting the environment, restricting the output and increasing the final price of the goods produced. There is a reduction in the benefit of consumers and corporate earnings.

In the second case, if the cost of abatement is sufficiently larger than the small disutility of pollution, then the government allows some emission of pollutants, thereby the costs of production will be reduced, which has a favorable impact on corporate profits and on the consumers' pocket.

And finally, in the third case, we consider the cost of abatement similar to marginal disutility of pollution. In this instance, the optimal environment policy depends on the efficiency level of the firms located in both countries. The country with more efficient firms will impose the severest restriction whilst the country with the less efficient firms will have less strict pollution restrictions (so, it will reduce of the production costs of firms promoting their competitiveness).

In regard to taxes, we have two cases. In both the magnitude of the optimal tax depends mainly on the size of the marginal disutility of pollution and on the number of local and foreign companies. In the first case, if the marginal disutility of pollution is sufficiently small, we can consider two subcases: 1) if the number of local firms is higher than the number of foreign firms, then the local government sacrifices the utility of the companies and the consumers benefit in exchange for the tax revenues from tax pollution, while the government of the foreign country subsidizes his firms, and 2) if the number of local and foreign firms are similar, both governments subsidize or otherwise exempt the taxes to their companies. This policy favors at the same time both producers and consumers in both countries, in exchange for a negligible increase in pollution levels. In the second case, when the marginal disutility of pollution is sufficiently large, the optimal policy is a tax in both countries. Moreover, the magnitude of both taxes may be different according to the number of firms located in each country.

Finally, both policies coincide in the case where the marginal disutility is very high, prioritizing the negative effect of pollution on the other components of the welfare function. In the case of quotas, minimizing the amount of allowed emissions, and in the case of taxes, imposing a high tax that discourages companies to pollute. Now, when the marginal disutility is not high enough, the policies applicable in the case of quotas and taxes are different. In the case of the quota, it depends on their relationship with the size of the abatement cost (with marginal disutility), but in the case of taxes, it depends on the majority of firms existing in each country.

In this way, the proposed model emphasizes the importance of establishing strategic rational environmental policies to act in two ways: on one hand, strengthening the competitiveness of firms and their surplus and the expected benefits for consumers, and on the other hand, choosing regulations that are conducive to obtaining sustainable development with a sustainable environment.

REFERENCES

Asako, K. (1979). Environmental pollution in an open economy. *Economic Record*, *55*(151), 359-367.

Balassa, B. (1966). Tariff reductions and trade in manufactures. *American Economic Review*, *56*, 466-473.

Brander, J. A. (1981). Intra-industry trade in identical commodities. *Journal of International Economics*, *11*, 1-14.

Brander, J A. & Krugman, P. (1983). A 'reciprocal dumping' model of international trade. *Journal of International Economics*, *15*, 313-321.

Caves, R. E. & Jones, R. W. (1977). *World trade and payments: an introduction* (2nd ed.). Boston: Little, Brown and Company.

Cropper, M. L. & Oates, W. E. (1992). Environmental economics: A survey. *Journal of Economic Literature*, *30*, 675-740.

Espinosa Ramírez, R. S. (2008). Reciprocal Dumping and Environmental Policies. *Panorama Económico*, *6*, 7-34.

IPCC (2007). *Contribution of Working Groups I, II and III to the Fourth Assessment Report of the Intergovernmental Panel on Climate Change*. Geneva, Switzerland: IPCC.

Krugman, P. (1979). Increasing returns, monopolistic competition and international trade. *Journal of International Economics*, 9, 469-479.

Lahiri, S. & Ono, Y. (1998). Protecting environment in the presence of foreign direct investment: tax versus quantity restriction. *mimeo* Department of Economics, University of Essex.

Lancaster, K. (1980). Intra-industry trade under perfect monopolistic competition. *Journal of International Economics*, *10*, 151-175.

Markusen, J. R., Morey, E. R. & Olewiler, N. (1993). Environmental policy when market structure and plant locations are endogenous. *Journal of Environmental Economics and Management*, *24*, 69-86.

Markusen, J. R., Morey, E. R. & Olewiler, N. (1995). Competition in regional environmental policies when plant locations are endogenous. *Journal of Public Economics*, *56*, 55-57.

In: Economics of Environmental Policy ... ISBN: 978-1-63463-165-5
Editors: M. G. Fikru and M. Insall

Chapter 4

INTER-INDUSTRY POLLUTION, COMPENSATION SCHEME AND ENVIRONMENTAL PROTECTION

***Leonard F.S. Wang*[1, *]*, Chu-chuan Hsu*[2] *and Tien-Der Han*[3]**

[1]Department of Applied Economics,
National University of Kaohsiung, Taiwan
[2]Department of Marketing and Logistics Management,
Yu Da University of Science and Technology, Taiwan
[3]School of Business and Economics,
Loughborough University, United Kingdom

ABSTRACT

This chapter discusses inter-industry pollution and corresponding environmental protection policies with the consideration of a budget constraint. We found that in the short run with no budget constraint, the output quantity based subsidy seriously distorts the price mechanism because the non-polluters will expand the production of output as much as possible to claim the subsidy, so that the profit can be maximized. Such a result raises the concerns for heavier fiscal burden and the

* Corresponding author: Leonard F. S. Wang, NUK Chair Professor, Department of Applied Economics, National University of Kaohsiung, No. 700, Kaohsiung University Road, Nan-Tzu District 811, Kaohsiung, Taiwan, R.O.C. Tel:886-7-5919322, Fax:886-7-5919320, E-mail address: lfswang@nuk.edu.tw.

unfairness of a society. When a budget constraint is considered to tackle the concerns, the government will pay the subsidy with caution and impose higher tax on the polluting firm. Thus the environmental protection is strengthened and the price mechanism distortion in the short run with no budget constraint is rectified. The arbitrarily high consumer surplus due to biased high output is also adjusted.

Keywords: Environmental Protection Policy, Compensation Scheme, Pollution Tax

1. INTRODUCTION

Environmental protection has been an important issue in recent years, especially after the 1970s. The Stockholm Declaration made by United Nations in 1972 was a milestone showing the world's awareness of the importance of the environmental protection. The Kyoto Protocol to the United Nations Framework Convention on Climate Change (UNFCCC) initiated in 1997 was the key worldwide collaboration to deal with the carbon dioxide emission. It was originally the only treaty that required by law the countries signing the treaty to reduce the greenhouse gas emissions to the stated level. It is an ongoing trend that more and more nationwide environmental protection policies and instruments are proposed to protect the domestic environment from being polluted (Bromley, 1995; Golub, 2003; Kamieniecki, 2012).

In the environmental economics literature, one major research strand focuses on the effects of tax or subsidy imposed on polluting firms (Bovenberg and Mooij, 1994; Bansal and Gangopadhyay, 2003; Fullerton and Heutel, 2007). The analyses have mainly focused on the welfare effect and/or the effects on pollution abatement. Nonetheless, it is noticeable that when pollution occurs, there are always victims of pollution. Consumers can suffer from pollution. Other firms can also be negatively affected by pollution. Nevertheless, rare attention has been paid to the compensation schemes that are designed for those negatively affected groups. There is, however, a strand of literature discussing the consumers with environmental protection awareness. The environmentally differentiated product model are adopted to conduct such research (Arora and Gangopadhyay, 1995; Moraga-González and Padrón-Fumero, 2002). In a similar line of research, Toshimitsu (2010) considers the consumer subsidy but focuses on the consumption subsidization when purchasing the environment friendly products.

As for the consideration of the external effects on other firms, Yin (2003) examines the effects of corrective taxes under oligopoly with inter-firm externalities and pollution abatement. The research shows that when externalities are substantial and/or the number of polluters is high, levies on effluent imposed on these firms do not necessarily end up with a deadweight loss. This kind of inter-firm pollution attracts much attention in the field of mixed oligopoly. It is because when a polluter is a publicly owned firm, it affects the determination of privatization policies as well as environmental protection policies and brings quite different policy effects (Bárcena-Ruiz and Garzón, 2002, 2006; Beladi and Chao, 2006; Wang and Wang, 2009). There is indeed also another important strand of literature focusing on the transboundary pollution (Taylor and Copeland, 1995; Wang and Chen, 2010). However, very few papers have deliberated how deterioration of production factors' productivity can affect environmental protection policies.

Moreover, when a compensation scheme is considered as part of environmental policies and the compensation is funded by a government, it is then essential to consider a fiscal burden of the government and the fairness of a society. Government fiscal burden is an important issue in recent years. It is obviously the case when the US government debt keeps soaring and makes the US government raise its public debt ceiling every year since 2006. The US government even partly shutdown in 2013. A budget constraint, therefore, should be a vital issue to consider when subsidization is included in policy design. This strand of literature on a budget constraint usually relates to public policy analyses (Choi, 2011; Ishida and Matsushima, 2009; Wang et al. 2013).

This chapter focuses on inter-industry pollution and considers not only environmental protection tax imposed on polluters but also subsidy paid to the negatively affected firms with the consideration of a budget constraint.

Despite that related research is rare, the inter-firm or even inter-industry pollution is as matter of fact very common in reality and can trigger serious controversy when the producing factors being polluted are hired by other firms. For example, laborers may have lower productivity when the air is polluted and almost all industries need laborers to produce goods or provide services. Beijing, the capital of China, is facing such pollution. The air pollution in Beijing is so severe that the Beijing city government is even considering pollution holidays. Some big enterprises are causing severe pollution and making its neighboring firms suffer from the productivity deterioration. In Taiwan, Formosa Petrochemical Corporation, the largest petrochemical corporation in Taiwan, generates adjudicated air and water pollution that cause the losses to fishermen and farmers for many times. The usual way to deal with a pollution incident is fine paid to the government and the reparation paid to the victims. However, there is lack of a systematically organized mechanism to handle the situation. It takes much effort of the victims to fight for recompense and the government usually helps the victims by providing a platform for both sides to negotiate. The government does not intervene the process of negotiation. Hence if it goes to a court, it requires the victims' time and energy to go through the whole process while the amount of amends is uncertain. Consequently, the victims have to pay a lot in advance, whereas the result remains unknown. If a government can act as an arbiter and use tax and subsidization to rectify the distortion, it might will be more effective in terms of environmental protection and social fairness. Moreover, if tax and subsidization are used to be the instruments to control pollution, it is not hard to understand the importance of a budget constraint.

The analysis begins with the environmental protection policy that no budget constraint is imposed to build a benchmark. Thereafter the budget constraint is considered into the model to proceed with the analysis. Optimal tax and subsidization rate as well as the amount of emission will be found out in both scenarios. Consumer surplus and the social welfare will also be revealed. Crucial comparisons will be made afterwards. Then this chapter shows the environmental protection policies and the role of a budget constraint as well as its effects on environmental protection.

The remainder of this chapter is organized as follows. Section 2 describes the model. Section 3 considers both short run and long run cases focusing on the environmental policies including tax and subsidy with no budget constraint. Section 4 considers a budget constraint and analyzes the corresponding environmental policies in the short run. Section 5 elaborates the effects of a budget constraint. Section 6 concludes.

2. The Model

There are two industries within a domestic market. One contains a monopolist firm generating pollution and causing damage to non-polluters that are in the other oligopolistic industry. This kind of relationship is often seen in reality. A few specific concrete examples are illustrated in the Introduction. The monopolistic firm and the firms in the oligopolistic industry deals with the following inverse demand, respectively

$$p_X = A - q_X$$
$$p_Y = A - \sum_{i=1}^{n} q_{iY}. \quad (1)$$

The subscript X and Y in the model represent the parameters considered in two industries, respectively. In the demand functions, p_X and p_Y are the prices in the two respective industries, and A stands for the market scale. The output of the polluter is q_X and the output of a non-polluter is q_{iY}. The cost structure of both types of firm are comprised of laborers hired and wage paid indicating $C_X = \mathrm{w}l_X$ and $C_y = \mathrm{w}l_Y$ where w is the wage paid to each laborer. To highlight the distortion caused by improper policy design, w is normalized to be 1 without loss of generality. Moreover, to tackle the problem of environmental pollution, a government not only imposes tax on the amount of residual pollutants generated from the production process of the polluter but also subsidizes the non-polluters for productivity losses that are caused by pollution. Hence the objective of the polluter is

$$\pi_X = p_X q_X - l_X - te_X - \frac{d(a_X)^2}{2} - k. \quad (2)$$

Due to the environmental protection policy, the polluter abates its amount of pollution by the amount of a_X. The government acknowledges the effort of the polluting firm, and thus environmental protection tax incurs only on the residual pollution e_X, and $e_X = q_X - a_X$. Therefore, the expenditure of the polluter spent on environmental protection tax is $T = te_X$, which is also the total tax revenue of the government. Moreover, to avoid an unreasonable situation that a government subsidizes residual pollution,[10] it is assumed that $d = 1$.

As for non-polluters, owing to the consideration of two scenarios, there are two types of objective function. When a budget constraint is not considered, a government subsidizes each non-polluter under the basis of its output quantity with the s units of subsidy per unit of output making total subsidy $S = \sum_{i=1}^{n} sq_{iY}$. Hence, the capital S indicates the total subsidy paid by the government.

$$\pi_{iY} = p_Y q_{iY} - l_{iY} - f + sq_{iY}. \quad (3)$$

[10] Because the environmental protection tax totals $T = te_X$, and when optimal tax t^* is negative, tax turns out to be subsidy indicating that the government subsidizes the polluter.

However, when a budget constraint is considered, the government will have incentive to control the amount of the total subsidy paid. The subsidization becomes the lump-sum subsidy making $S = ns$. Thus the objective function of a non-polluter is

$$\pi_{iY} = p_Y q_{iY} - l_{iY} - f + s. \tag{4}$$

Note that in the model there are two policies considered: tax and subsidy. Both of these are environmental policies and no other tax on consumption or profit exists. To specify the efficiency losses brought by inter-industry pollution, the laborer productivity of the non-polluters is $l_{iY}/q_{iY} = 1/(1+\beta e_X)$, $\beta > 0$ while that of the polluter is $l_X/q_X = 1$. It indicates that the polluting firm needs one unit of laborer to produce one unit of output and a non-polluter needs more than one unit of laborer to produce one unit of output on accounts of the productivity deterioration caused by pollution. Therefore, β measures the magnitude of inter-industry pollution and when $\beta = 0$, there is no inter-industry pollution. Lastly, entry costs are set to be k and f where k stands for the entry cost of the polluter and f represents the entry cost of a non-polluter.

Consequently, the social welfare can be defined as the summation of consumer surplus, producer surplus, tax collected, subsidy paid and residual pollution generated. The residual pollution is defined as $ED = g\,(e_X)^2/2$ standing for the total damage of pollution. When $g > 0$, the detriment caused by pollution is not only the productivity deterioration of the other industry but also the overall social welfare reduction. The consumer surplus is represented by CS. Resulting from the linear demand function, the consumer surplus is $CS = {Q_X^2}/{2} + {Q_Y^2}/{2}$ where Q_X^2 and Q_Y^2 indicate the total output of the polluting industry and the polluted industry, respectively.

To focus on the main purpose of this chapter, it is assumed that $g = 1$ and $\beta = 1$. Hence, when a budget constraint is not considered, the social welfare is revealed in Eq. (5) while the social welfare under the consideration of the budget constraint is unveiled in Eq. (6).

$$SW = CS_X + \sum_{i=1}^{n} CS_{iY} + \pi_X + \sum_{i=1}^{n} \pi_{iY} + te_X - s\sum_{i=1}^{n} q_{iY} - \frac{(e_X)^2}{2} \tag{5}$$

$$SW = CS_X + \sum_{i=1}^{n} CS_{iY} + \pi_X + \sum_{i=1}^{n} \pi_{iY} + te_X - \sum_{i=1}^{n} s_i \quad - \frac{(e_X)^2}{2}$$
$$\text{s.t. } \left(te_X - \sum_{i=1}^{n} s_i \ \right) = 0. \tag{6}$$

The model is a two-stage game. At the second stage, the non-polluters compete with quantity. In the first stage, the government decides the environmental protection policy including tax collected from the polluter and the subsidy paid to the non-polluters. Through backward induction, the equilibrium is calculated.

3. Policy Decisions with No Budget Constraint

This section highlights the concerns proposed in the beginning that if environmental protection tax does not suffice to offset the subsidy payment from the government, then it is identical to that the whole society funds the polluter to compensate the firms that are negatively affected by pollution. It is on grounds that tax collected from the polluter should on one hand incentivize the polluter to abate pollution. On the other hand, tax ought to be enough to be used as subsidy to recompense the non-polluters or the government will have extra fiscal burden to deal with the overall pollution issue.

First subsection focuses on the short run analysis while the second subsection extends the analysis to the long run.

3.1. Policy Decisions with No Budget Constraint in the Short Run

In the second stage, the firms choose their output under the consideration of pollution abatement to maximize their profit. Therefore, using Eqs. (2) and (3), the first order conditions of their objective functions are[11]

$$\frac{\partial \pi_X}{\partial a_X} = t - a_X = 0$$

$$\frac{\partial \pi_X}{\partial q_X} = A - 2q_X - 1 - t = 0$$

[11] The second-conditions are $\frac{\partial^2 \pi_X}{\partial a_X^2} = -1 < 0$, $\frac{\partial^2 \pi_X}{\partial q_X^2} = -2 < 0$, and $\frac{\partial \pi_{iY}}{\partial q_{iY}} = -(n+1) < 0$ satisfying the sufficient condition for the maxima.

$$\frac{\partial \pi_{iY}}{\partial q_{iY}} = A - (n+1)q_{iY} - (1 - a_X + q_X) + s = 0$$

Solving the equation set simultaneously delivers the results in the second stage including pollutants abated and profit maximization output as shown in the following equations, respectively

$$a_X = t$$

$$q_X = \frac{1}{2}(A - t - 1)$$

$$q_{iY} = \frac{A+2s+3t-1}{2(n+1)}$$

Then based on the results of the pollutants abated and the output quantity derived in the second stage, the government decides its environmental protection policy. Through the maximization of social welfare defined in Eq. (5) the optimal tax and subsidy rate is determined as

$$t^* = \frac{1}{7}(A - 2) \tag{7}$$

$$s^* = A\left(\frac{2}{7} + \frac{1}{n}\right) + \frac{13}{14} \tag{8}$$

Note that the super-script * hereafter indicates the equilibrium values calculated after the optimal policies are obtained. Given the equilibrium tax and the subsidy rates, the equilibrium pollution abatement, output of the polluter and a non-polluter are, respectively,

$$\begin{aligned} a_X^* &= \frac{1}{7}(A - 2) \\ q_X^* &= \frac{1}{14}(6A - 5) \\ q_{iY}^* &= \frac{A}{n} \end{aligned} \tag{9}$$

The equilibrium residual pollution can be found as

$$e_X^* = \frac{1}{14}(4A - 1) \tag{10}$$

Then total tax collected and subsidy paid are

$$T^* = \frac{1}{98}(A-2)(4A-1) \tag{11}$$

$$S^* = \frac{1}{14}A[A\left(4+\frac{14}{n}\right)+13] \tag{12}$$

It is immediate that the subsidy paid outweighs tax collected because

$$T^* - S^* = \frac{n-A[50n+A(49+12n)]}{49n} < 0 \tag{13}$$

Hence the following Lemma summarizes the first important finding:

Lemma 1: *When inter-industry pollution exists and causes the productivity deterioration of the polluted industry, if subsidy is provided under the basis of the output quantity, the environmental protection tax revenue collected from the polluter does not suffice to offset the payment of the total subsidy.*

Through the equilibrium quantity of the output, the equilibrium price of the two industries can be found as

$$P_X^* = \frac{1}{14}(8A+5) \tag{14}$$

$$P_Y^* = 0 \tag{15}$$

From such a result, it can be understood that without proper design, a government's policy can cause even more distortion to an economy, which is also known as government failure. It is true that pollution is eased because of tax imposed, and subsidy is also paid to compensate the losses of the non-polluters. However, without proper design, such a policy is actually resulting in a worse consequence because tax collected from the polluter does not suffice for the total subsidy. It is to say that the whole society is paying for the polluter to compensate the non-polluters. Not to mention the distortion of the market mechanism the policy brings.

To see how the policy distorts the market mechanism, it is vital to understand that although normalizing wage to 1 is extreme, it helps to point out the outcomes of an inappropriately designed policy. When the marginal cost of the non-polluters is lower than the subsidy rate, the subsidy turns out to be a strong distortion making the firms maximize their output to claim the subsidy as much as possible, so that the profit is maximized and makes the equilibrium price decline to an unreasonably low level. The market mechanism is thus seriously distorted. This result can be understood from the price of the polluted industry, as indicated in Eq. (15), and the profit of a non-polluter shown in Eq. (17) below. The following equations illustrate the profit of the polluting firm and the non-polluters. Note that even if the market price of the polluted industry is zero, the non-polluters are still making positive profit.

$$\pi_X^* = \frac{1}{196}(38A^2 - 68A + 33) - k \tag{16}$$

$$\pi_{iY}^* = \frac{A^2}{n^2} - f \tag{17}$$

Hence, the following proposition is immediate.

Proposition 1 *When inter-industry pollution deteriorates factor productivity of a non-polluter that is in an industry being polluted, if subsidy is provided under the basis of output quantity and the marginal cost of non-polluters are sufficiently low, the subsidization seriously distorts the price mechanism.*

3.2. Policy Decisions with No Budget Constraint in the Long Run

This subsection extends the short run result in the last subsection to the long run to see if higher flexibility of the market will make any difference. When in the long run, the non-polluters are able to enter and exit the market freely. The firms will enter the market until the profit is zero. Under such a circumstance, the market becomes more flexible.

With the same subsidization policy design and using the same techniques in the last subsection, it can be derived that, in the second stage, the pollutant abatement, output quantity, and the number of firms are, respectively,

$$a_X = t \tag{18}$$

$$q_X = \frac{1}{2}(A - t - 1) \tag{19}$$

$$q_{iY} = \sqrt{f} \tag{20}$$

$$n = \frac{2(A+s-\sqrt{f})-(A-3t+2)+1}{2\sqrt{f}} \tag{21}$$

Then through the former result, the optimal environmental protection tax rate and the subsidy rate can be obtained as

$$t^* = \frac{1}{7}(A-2) \tag{22}$$

$$s^* = \frac{2A}{7} + \frac{13}{14} \tag{23}$$

It is clear that tax rate imposed on the polluter in the long run and in the short run are the same. It is because tax charged is based on the amount of residual pollution and there is no incentive making the polluter change the level of its pollution abatement. As for subsidy, the subsidy paid to each non-polluter is not comparable between the short run and the long run cases. It results from that in the long run the firms can enter and exit the market freely but in the short run the number of firms is fixed. However, in the short run, due to that the equilibrium subsidy rate is $s^* = A\left(\frac{2}{7}+\frac{1}{n}\right)+\frac{13}{14}$, the more the non-polluters are, the lower the subsidy rate will be. In turn, it reduces the subsidy rate difference between the short run and the long run.

Knowing tax and subsidy rate, the equilibrium pollution abatement, residual pollution and output can be found as

$$a_X^* = \frac{1}{7}(A-2) \tag{24}$$

$$e_X^* = \frac{1}{14}(4A-1) \tag{25}$$

$$q_X^* = \frac{1}{14}(6A-5) \tag{26}$$

$$q_{iY}^* = \sqrt{f} \tag{27}$$

Then through the equilibrium output as well as tax and subsidy rates obtained, the equilibrium total tax and subsidy are, respectively,

$$T^* = \frac{1}{98}(A-2)(4A-1) \tag{28}$$

$$S^* = \frac{1}{14}(13 + 4A)(A - \sqrt{f}) \tag{29}$$

The difference between the total tax collected and the total subsidy paid is as follows.

$$T^* - S^* = \frac{1}{98}\left[7(13 + 4A)\sqrt{f} - 4A(25 + 6A) + 2\right] < 0 \ \ if\ f > 0 \tag{30}$$

Since the entry cost is represented by f ensuring $f > 0$, it is clear that when in the long run, the environmental protection tax revenue is still not enough for the payment of the subsidy. Hence the following Proposition summarizes the short run findings proved in previous subsection and the long run findings disclosed in Lemma 1.

Proposition 2 *When inter-industry pollution deteriorates factor productivity of a non-polluter that is in an industry being polluted, if the subsidy is provided under the basis of the output quantity, the total environmental protection tax revenue does not suffice to offset the total subsidy payment in both short run and long run.*

The equilibrium price of both products are revealed in the following equations.

$$P_X^* = \frac{1}{14}(8A + 5) \tag{31}$$

$$P_Y^* = \sqrt{f} \tag{32}$$

This outcome points out the abused use of subsidy is eliminated by competition. In the long run, firms are free to enter and exit the market, which means that the firms are facing more intensified competition and the subsidy obtained from the government is not enough to support the firms to survive.

After finding out the equilibrium price, output, tax and subsidy, the profit of both type of firms can be determined.

$$\pi_X^* = \frac{1}{196}(38A^2 - 68A + 33) - k \tag{33}$$

$$\pi_{iY}^* = 0 \tag{34}$$

4. POLICY DECISIONS WITH A BUDGET CONSTRAINT IN THE SHORT RUN

The former section deliberates that proper policy collaboration is essential. Environmental protection tax is to rectify pollution caused. To fix the issue of market failure, when there are victims of pollution, they should be compensated, and thus subsidy is essential. It is because in reality it is difficult and costly for those negatively affected groups to deal with polluters, especially when the polluter is a large enterprise. Nonetheless, when tax and subsidy are both implemented to correct the distortion brought by pollution, it can be an issue that when environmental protection tax collected by the government is not enough to pay the subsidy, let alone those more serious distorting effects brought by the improperly designed policies in the short run. A budget constraint may be one way to neutralize the effects of pollution, environmental protection policies and the compensation scheme.

First of all, total subsidy to be paid needs to be constrained within the total revenue of environmental protection tax. Second, to avoid the abused use of subsidy, the type of subsidy is changed from the output quantity based subsidy to lump-sum subsidy. Therefore, through Eqs. (2) and (4), the firms choose their profit maximization output under the consideration of pollution abatement in the second stage as

$$a_X = t$$

$$q_X = \frac{1}{2}(A - t - 1)$$

$$q_{iY} = \frac{A+(3t-1)}{2(n+1)}$$

Then based on the quantity decided in the second stage, the government decides tax and subsidy to maximize social welfare. The social welfare is

$$SW = -\frac{1}{8(1+n)^2}[2 + n(4 + 3n) - A^2(2 + n(8 + 5n)) + 2A(n(2 + n)(1 - 5t) - 2t) + 8t + 2n(8 + n)t + (14 + n(28 + 23n))t^2] - k - nf$$
$$\text{s.t } \left(te_X - \textstyle\sum_{i=1}^{n} s_i\right) = 0 \qquad (35)$$

Through Lagrange method, Eq. (35) can be arranged as

$$L = SW + \lambda\left(te_X - \sum_{i=1}^{n} s_i\right)$$

Then, following two equations illustrate the equilibrium tax, t^*, collected from the polluter per unit of residual pollution and the subsidy, s^*, paid to each non-polluter.

$$t^* = \frac{A[5n(n+2)+2]-n(n+8)-4}{n(23n+28)+14} \tag{36}$$

$$s^* = \frac{[A(5n(n+2)+2)-n(n+8)-4][A(n(4n-1)+4)-2n(5n+1)-1]}{n[n(23n+28)+14]^2} \tag{37}$$

Note that $T \equiv te_X$ and $S \equiv \sum_{i=1}^{n} s_i$ and to achieve the budget constraint, it is required that $T^* - S^* = 0$ in equilibrium. Hence, the total tax collected and the total subsidy paid are, respectively

$$T^* = S^* = \frac{[A(5n(n+2)+2)-n(n+8)-4][A(n(4n-1)+4)-2n(5n+1)-1]}{[n(23n+28)+14]^2} \tag{38}$$

With the equilibrium tax and subsidy, the equilibrium pollution abatement, residual pollution, and equilibrium output can be calculated as

$$a_X^* = \frac{A[5n(n+2)+2]-n(n+8)-4}{n(23n+28)+14} \tag{39}$$

$$e_X^* = \frac{A[n(4n-1)+4]-2n(5n+1)-1}{n(23n+28)+14} \tag{40}$$

$$q_X^* = \frac{A[9n(n+1)+6]-n(11n+10)-5}{n(23n+28)+14} \tag{41}$$

$$q_{iY}^* = \frac{A(19n+10)-13(n+1)}{n(23n+28)+14} \tag{42}$$

It is also derived that the equilibrium price of the polluting and the polluted industries are, respectively

$$P_X^* = \frac{A[n(14n+19)+8]+n(11n+10)+5}{n(23n+28)+14} \tag{43}$$

$$P_Y^* = \frac{(n+1)[2A(2n+7)+13n]}{n(23n+28)+14} \tag{44}$$

When comparing the equilibrium price derived here and that of the polluted industry illustrated in the last subsection, it can be realized that with restricted compensation, non-polluters are not able to misuse the subsidy. The subsidized firms will not expand the output without limit and make the price drop to an unreasonably low level to claim the subsidy but take the market price into consideration. Thus

Corollary 1 *When inter-industry pollution deteriorates factor productivity of a non-polluter that is in an industry being polluted, a budget constraint is able to rectify the distorted price mechanism brought by output quantity based pollution subsidization.*

5. Effects of a Budget Constraint in the Short Run

According to the Section 3, tax collected does not suffice for the subsidy in both short run and long run. It implies that government failure and the concern for higher fiscal burden and social fairness should not be neglected. Hence, the need of a budget constraint can be easily understood. Therefore, this section deliberates the impacts of a budget constraint. In the following discussion, the superscript *c* indicates the scenario with a budget constraint, whereas *nc* means the scenario with no budget constraint. The comparisons are made under the short run basis.

The first important finding is that the polluting firm has to bear a heavier burden of environmental protection tax. Using tax under the consideration of a budget constraint minus that under no budget constraint shows

$$t^c - t^{nc} = a^c - a^{nc} = \frac{3n[2A(2n+7)+13n]}{7[n(23n+28)+14]} > 0 \tag{45}$$

When the environmental protection tax becomes higher, it motivates the polluter to devote more efforts to deal with its pollution. From the comparison of the pollutant abated within the two scenarios illustrated in Eq. (45), it can be seen that the budget constraint makes the environmental protection even better. Better environmental protection is also verified by the reduction of residual pollutant. In Eq. (46), e_X^c stands for pollution abatement under the consideration of the budget constraint and e_X^{nc} represents pollution abatement under no budget constraint. The residual pollutants emitted becomes fewer as Eq. (46) indicates.

$$e_X^c - e_X^{nc} = -\frac{9n[2A(2n+7)+13n]}{14[n(23n+28)+14]} < 0 \tag{46}$$

Proposition 3 *When inter-industry pollution deteriorates factor productivity of a non-polluter that is in an industry being polluted, a budget constraint can strengthen environmental protection.*

Comparing the total subsidy paid to non-polluters under two scenarios shows that without the budget constraint, a government is willing to subsidize more as shown below

$$\begin{aligned} S^c - S^{nc} = (&-1836A^2n^5 - 12068A^2n^4 - 23492A^2n^3 - 22596A^2n^2 \\ &- 11648A^2n - 2744A^2 - 7633An^5 - 18718An^4 \\ &- 19362An^3 - 10780An^2 - 2800An + 140n^5 + 1148n^4 \\ &+ 798n^3 + 224n^2 + 56n)/[14 + n(28+23n)]^2 < 0 \end{aligned} \tag{47}$$

It is worth mentioning that not only the total subsidy is reduced, the subsidy paid to each non-polluter also decreases.

$$\begin{aligned} &s^c - s^{nc} \\ &= \frac{[A(5n(n+2)+2) - n(n+8) - 4][A(n(4n-1)+4) - 2n(5n+1) - 1]}{n(n(23n+28)+14)^2} \\ &- A(\frac{1}{n} + \frac{2}{7}) - \frac{13}{14} < 0 \end{aligned} \tag{48}$$

This result can be inferred a little further that when a government is subsidizing an industry but without proper subsidization policy design, it is very easy and even tempting for firms in the industry to abuse the subsidy. It is exactly what has been proved within this chapter that the subsidized firms treat the subsidy as the main profit source by means of producing unreasonably high volume of output to claim the subsidy and causes the price drop to a very low level.

Knowing that tax becomes higher and the environmental protection is better, following equations reveal the profit difference of firms under two scenarios. The former illustrates the profit of the polluting firm while the latter shows that of a non-polluter.

$$\pi_X^c - \pi_X^{nc} = -\frac{3n[2A(2n+7)+13n][2A(n(74n+49)+56] - n(163n+56)-28)}{196(n(23n+28)+14)^2} < 0 \; if \; A > 1 \tag{49}$$

$$\pi_{iY}^c - \pi_{iY}^{nc} = \frac{2A^2(n(n(2n(5n+99)+199)+69)+4) - A(n(n(n(54n+635)+811)+302)+18) + n(n(n(10n+251)+395)+185)+4}{n(n(23n+28)+14)^2} - \frac{A^2}{n^2} < 0 \tag{50}$$

The profit of both type of firms are lower when the budget constraint is imposed. To the polluter, because tax is higher making it devote more effort to reduce its pollution, its profit then decreases. As in the profit function of the polluting firm, it can also be seen that the more the pollutants are reduced, the lower the profit will be.

As for non-polluters, in the scenario of output quantity based subsidy, the main source of the profit is subsidy. However, when the subsidization mechanism transforms to the lump sum subsidy, the profit source of non-polluters turns back to product selling via market competition. It is to say that in the no budget constraint scenario, the competition among firms does not affect the profitability of firms much, whereas in the scenario with the budget constraint the competition becomes the main force that determines the behaviors of the firms. As described in the subsection 3.1, the non-polluters will produce as much as possible owing to that the firms can exploit the output they produce to claim the subsidy and when lacking in the budget constraint, a government is willing to subsidize more. However, it is not the case in the scenario with a budget constraint and lump sum subsidy.

In brevity, in the scenario with the output quantity based subsidy, the gain from the subsidy can outweigh the profit from the market is mainly because of the subsidization policy design, and the side effect of the policy is the main power that distorts the price mechanism.

To consumers, the differences of consumer surplus under two different scenarios can be found in the following equation.

$$\begin{aligned} & CS^c - CS^{nc} \\ & = -\frac{[13n + 2A(7 + 2n)][-n(2968 + n(5936 + 3355n)] + 2A[1372 + n(5348 + n(8281 + 4512n))]}{392(14 + n(28 + 23n))^2} \\ & < 0 \end{aligned} \quad (51)$$

It is not a surprise that consumer surplus becomes worse off under the consideration of the budget constraint. It is on grounds that within the scenario of no budget constraint, non-polluters would expand their output quantity as much as possible, so that the most subsidy can be obtained, and thus the profit is maximized. However, in the scenario with a budget constraint, a government subsidizes non-polluters with caution, and thus the firms are not able rely on the subsidy that much. Therefore, the firms will not produce without limit making the price too low. Consequently, the equilibrium output is lower and the equilibrium price is higher when there is a budget constraint and consumers then suffer.

Actually, it is the government that encourages the subsidized firms to produce more and consumers become beneficiaries. A non-polluter's marginal cost, the wage paid to laborers, is not increasing along with the increase of the output. Consequently, as long as the subsidy rate is higher than the marginal cost, the subsidized firms will have a strong incentive to expand the output. Since the marginal cost is not increasing with the output, there is no counter effect to make the subsidized firms limit their output, and thus the market price is driven to a very low level. Hence, consumer surplus is maximized but in an unhealthy way that shifts all producer surplus to consumers. Letting the marginal cost be a constant is a strong assumption, but in reality it is also true when the main producing factor is laborers.

Lastly, the change of the social welfare is unveiled below.

$$SW^c - SW^{nc} = -\frac{[2A(2n + 7) + 13n]^2}{28[n(23n + 28) + 14]} < 0 \quad (52)$$

The social welfare is worse off. It is also not a surprise that the social welfare deteriorates. It is due to that although the problem of pollution and the fiscal burden are eased, the improvement is at the cost of the profit of firms and consumer surplus.

Nevertheless, we are not saying that imposing a budget constraint is inappropriate. On the contrary, a budget constraint provides an opportunity to rectify the distortion. In terms of social welfare, the budget constraint is indeed cost but the budget constraint not only fixes the problem of the price mechanism distortion brought by the subsidization policy but also strengthens the environment protection. The losses consist of consumer surplus deterioration and profit dropping of both type of firms, but such a comparison is made under a distorted basis. The distorted basis indicates non-polluters' subsidy misuse and thereby the arbitrarily high consumer surplus. Not to mention that the profit decrease of the polluter is owing to that it devotes more to pollution abatement, and thus making the profit lower.

Proposition 4 *When inter-industry pollution deteriorates factor productivity of a non-polluter that is in an industry being polluted, a budget constraint worsens the profit of firms, consumer surplus and social welfare but such a short run comparison is made under a distorted basis with no budget constraint.*

CONCLUSION

Environmental protection has been an important issue since the 1970s. Numerous research has been conducted to explore various environment related fields. However, very few papers have paid attention to the inter-industry pollution while inter-industry pollution is an often seen phenomenon nowadays. Thus, this chapter aims to extend understanding of the inter-industry pollution with the consideration of a budget constraint.

In the model, there is one monopolist industry that inflicts pollution on the other oligopolistic industry, which deteriorates the productivity of the polluted industry. Hence, the firms in the latter suffer from losses. Moreover, one crux of the analysis lies in demonstrating the role of a budget constraint. The budget constraint requires that pollution tax revenue suffice for compensating the losses of non-polluters. Hence, the government plays a pivotal role that guarantees the realization of compensation and simultaneously protects the environment, and thus the market failure can be fixed. Therefore, the environmental protection policy is comprised of the pollution abatement policy and the compensation scheme. Such an environmental protection policy aims at mitigating the problem of environmental pollution and ensuring the fulfillment of compensation while keeping the fiscal burden of a government from increasing. It is important to realize that if pollution tax revenue is not enough for the compensation payment, then implicitly it is tantamount that all tax payers subsidize the polluter to compensate the non-polluters, and explicitly the fiscal burden of the government becomes heavier. In the model, laborers are the production factor of the firms in both industries. Due to that the monopolistic polluting firm in one industry generates pollutants that deteriorate the laborer productivity of the firms in the other industry, the firms being negatively affected undergo the production losses. Such inter-industry pollution are countless. The Introduction illustrates a few specific concrete examples.

In the scenario with no budget constrain, both analyses in the short run and in the long run are considered. In the short run, the subsidy paid to each non-polluter is according to the output quantity of that firm. The subsidized firms will then take advantage of the subsidy to maximize the profit by means of expanding its output volume as much as possible, so that the firm can claim higher subsidy to maximize the profit. However, such a behavior brings the market price to an unreasonably low level and seriously distorts the price mechanism, and thus government failure occurs. Nonetheless, the low price and high output benefit consumers but in an extremely distorted way. Moreover, the total tax revenue collected does not suffice to offset the total payment of the subsidy.

In the long run with the same subsidization scheme and economic environment, non-polluters are able to enter and exit the market freely. Hence, the non-polluters are facing intensified competition, and the subsidy is not enough to support the firms' survival. The firms then reduce the output, and thus the price rises but total subsidy paid still outweigh tax collected. Though the environmental protection is not worse off, it is not better off either. The short run and long run analyses show that a government needs to alter the policy design to rectify at least the problem of insufficient tax revenue and the market mechanism distorted subsidization scheme.

In the short run, putting a budget constraint into consideration and changing the output quantity based subsidy to lump sum subsidy is a possible way to fix the aforementioned problems. When a budget constraint is considered, a government will have an incentive to pay the subsidy with caution, and thus changing the subsidization policy to lump sum subsidy becomes an alternative. Meanwhile, a government will re-consider the environmental protection tax rate to meet the requirement of the budget constraint.

When the subsidization scheme becomes lump sum subsidy, the subsidized firms can no longer rely on the subsidy to make profit. Consequently, the government failure and the market distortion brought by the quantity based subsidy are rectified. The budget constraint, together with the lump sum subsidy, raises the environmental protection tax rate, and thus the environmental protection is enhanced.

However, it is worthwhile to point out that, when a budget constraint is considered, consumers, the polluting firm and the non-polluters are all worse off. It is on grounds that in the scenario with no budget constraint, the consumer surplus are arbitrarily high. Therefore, when the distortion is fixed, the consumers need to bear with the rectification. The polluting firm also suffers from lower profit. It is because the environmental protection tax rate are raised, which incentivizes the polluter to devote more effort to pollution abatement and it is costly to do so. Lastly, non-polluters are also worse off. It results from less subsidy, even though the problem of pollution is eased. Consequently, the social welfare deteriorates when a budget constraint is imposed, but it is paramount to understand that this deterioration is derived from a comparison made under a distorted basis.

This research is still limited in some aspects. The seriousness of subsidy distortion is related to the cost structure of the subsidized firm. It is not the purpose of this research but should be interesting to figure out the optimal subsidization policy when facing different cost structures. Moreover, the wage in this research is exogenously given and when unions are considered, the environmental protection policy and subsidization policy can be very different. Lastly, in a more realistic scenario, there is no deny that a non-polluter still has a chance to successfully litigate against a polluter and claim for compensation when the compensation scheme designed in this research is implemented. If it is the case, there will be a double punishment imposed on the polluter. It then probably stimulates the polluter to over abate its pollution in terms of overall social welfare and causes resources misallocation. It is because due to the double punishment the polluter will have stronger incentive to abate pollution further and allocates more resources to realize it. Hence the polluter's other economic activities including products producing can be crowed out, and thus resources misallocation occurs. This inference is important and worth further exploration.

REFERENCES

Arora, S. & Gangopadhyay, S. (1995). "Toward a Theoretical Model of Voluntary Over-Compliance" *Journal of Economic Behavior and Organization*, *28*, 289-309.

Bansal, S. & Gangopadhyay, S. (2003). "Tax/subsidy Policies in the Presence of Environmentally Aware Consumers" *Journal of Environmental Economics and Management*, *45*, 333-355.

Bárcena-Ruiz, J. C. & Garzón, M. B. (2002). "Environmental Taxes and Strategic Delegation" *Spanish Economic Review*, *4*, 301-310.

Bárcena-Ruiz, J. C. & Garzón, M. B. (2006). "Mixed Oligopoly and Environmental Policy" *Spanish Economic Review*, *8*, 139-160.

Beladi, H. & Chao, C. C. (2006). "Does Privatization Improve the Environment?" *Economics Letters*, *93*, 343-347.

Bromley, D. W. (1995). *The Handbook of Environmental Economics*, Oxford: Blackwell Publishers.

Bovenberg, A. L. & de Mooij, R. A. (1994). "Environmental Levies and Distortionary Taxation" *American Economic Review*, *84*, 1080-1089.

Choi, K. (2011). "Strategic Budget Constraints in a Unionized Mixed Oligopoly" *Japanese Economic Review*, *62*, 504-516.

Fullertona, D. & Heutel, G. (2007). "The General Equilibrium Incidence of Environmental Taxes" *Journal of Public Economics*, *91*, 571-591.

Golub, J. (2003). *New Instruments for Environmental Policy in the EU*. New York: Routledge.

Ishida, J. & Matsushima, N. (2009). "Should Civil Servants Be Restricted in Wage Bargaining? A Mixed-Duopoly Approach" *Journal of Public Economics*, *93*, 634-646.

Kamieniecki, S. & Kraft, M. (2012). *The Oxford Handbook of U.S. Environmental Policy*. New York: Oxford.

Moraga-González, J. L. & Padrón-Fumero, N. (2002). "Environmental Policy in a Green Market" *Environmental and Resource Economics*, *22*, 419-447.

Taylor, M. S. & Copeland, B. R. (1995). "Trade and Transboundary Pollution" *American Economic Review*, *85*, 716-737.

Toshimitsu, T. (2010). "On the Paradoxical Case of a Consumer-Based Environmental Subsidy Policy" *Economic Modelling*, *27*, 159-164.

Yin, X. (2003). "Corrective Taxes under Oligopoly with Inter-Firm Externalities" *Environmental and Resource Economics*, *26*, 269-277.

Wang, L. F. S. & Chen, T. L. (2010). "Trade Liberalization and Transboundary Pollution in an International Mixed Duopoly" *Environmental Economics and Policy Studies*, *12*, 187-200.

Wang, L. F. S., Hsu, C. C. & Lee, J. Y. (2013). "Do Partial Cross Ownership and Budget Constraints Matter for Privatization Policy" *Journal of Industry, Competition and Trade*, Forthcoming.

Wang, L. F. S. & Wang, J. (2009). "Environmental Taxes in a Differentiated Mixed Duopoly" *Economic System*, *33*, 389-396.

In: Economics of Environmental Policy … ISBN: 978-1-63463-165-5
Editors: M. G. Fikru and M. Insall

Chapter 5

Emission Tax and Acquisition Incentives in Oligopoly Markets

Mahelet G. Fikru * ***and Matt Insall***
Missouri University of Science and Technology, MO, US

Abstract

Even though most acquisitions take place among manufacturing firms regulated by environmental policies, there are not many studies which model acquisition decisions when such policies are present. In this book chapter, we model acquisition incentives when polluting firms compete in a Cournot oligopoly market. Our result suggests that emission tax can affect acquisition decisions. The exact relationship between emission tax and acquisition (dis)incentives depends on the pollution intensity of the potential acquisition partners. Furthermore our findings suggest that there may be perverse incentive situations, namely cases in which dirtier firms profitably acquire cleaner firms without making use of their cleaner technology.

1. Introduction

Even though most acquisitions take place among firms regulated by environmental policies, there are not many studies which model acquisition

* Corresponding author: fikruma@mst.edu.

decisions when such policies are present. Currently the Environmental Protection Agency (EPA) of the United States of America (USA) has proposed a state-based carbon tax to reduce emissions (Brookings, 2014). Among other sectors of the economy, the manufacturing, utility and transportation sectors are expected to experience a rise in cost of production which would lead to higher prices (Congressional Budget Office, 2013). These sectors have historically frequently engaged in merger and acquisition deals. For instance, in 2013 in the USA a total of 97 merger and acquisition deals were announced in the utilities sector with a combined value of over $22 billion (authors' calculation based on Thomson Reuter M&A deals dataset).

How would an emission tax, such as a carbon tax, affect acquisition incentives, if at all? This paper builds a simple oligopoly market model to understand the effect of emission tax on acquisition incentive. We build upon previous studies which use a theoretical model to link acquisition incentives to environmental externalities (Fikru and Insall, 2014; Fikru, 2013; Fikru, 2014; and Fikru and Lahiri, 2013).

Our finding, though not general, indicates that there is a possibility for perverse incentives, in the sense that the consequences of a given policy may be antithetical to its original intent. Our result suggests that emission tax can affect acquisition decisions. The exact relationship between emission tax and acquisition (dis)incentives depends on the pollution intensity of the potential acquisition partners. We have found cases in which an increase in emission tax is directly related to the acquisition incentive.

Section 2 presents the theoretical model. In section 2.1 we state some simplifying assumptions; in section 2.2 we solve for the Cournot solution and in section 2.3 we derive some conditions that lead to a profitable acquisition. Section 3 presents a special case and discusses implications. Finally section 4 concludes the chapter and puts forth some questions for future studies.

2. Basic Model

In this section, we first set up the theoretical model framework and discuss some simplifying assumptions. Our theoretical model is adopted from Fikru (2013), Fikru (2014), Fikru and Lahiri (2013) and Fikru and Insall (2014). We then present profit maximization solutions and discuss parameters that affect acquisition incentives.

2.1. Assumptions

There are four firms producing a homogenous good and competing in a Cournot oligopoly market. The market demand for the good is linear and given as $p = a - X$ where $X = x_1 + x_2 + x_3 + x_4$ and $a > 0$. x_i is the output of firm i (i =*1, 2 ,3, 4*), X is the market quantity demanded and p is the consumer price of the good. The marginal cost of production is assumed to be zero for each firm.

Firms use an end-of-the-pipe-type abatement technology where initially production results in gross pollution out of which the firm abates a certain amount while the rest is emitted (Fikru, 2013; Fikru, 2014; Fikru and Lahiri, 2013). Gross pollution is proportional to output level.

$$A_i = \theta(x_i) - e_i$$
$$\theta(x_i) = Z_i x_i \text{ where } Z_i > 0 \qquad (1)$$

A_i is the abatement level of firm i, $\theta(x_i)$ is gross pollution, Z_i is the pollution intensity of firm i and e_i is the emission level of firm i. For example, e_i can be tons of CO_2 *released* by firm i and Z_i can be tons of CO_2 *produced* per unit of output. Firms with a lower Z_i have low-carbon intensive production while firms with high Z_i have high carbon-intensive production. Since firms produce identical products, the industry pollution intensity is given by H where $H = Z_1 + Z_2 + Z_3 + Z_4$. We take the special case where $H = 10$, thus the industry's pollution intensity is 10 tons of CO_2 per unit of output.

All firms are penalized for their emission and they are required to pay a per unit emission tax of t where t is strictly positive. The cost function for abating pollution, $g(A_i)$, is assumed to be quadratic in the abatement level. That is, $g(A_i) = A_i^2/2$.

2.2. Cournot Solutions

Each firm maximizes profit with respect to output and emission level as follows

$$\max_{x_i, e_i} \pi_i = px_i - g(A_i) - te_i \tag{2}$$

The first order profit maximization conditions yield the following equilibrium values where * denotes a value at equilibrium

$$\begin{aligned} x_i^* &= \frac{a + 10t - 5tZ_i}{5} \\ p^* &= \frac{a + 10t}{5} \\ A_i^* &= t \\ \pi_i^* &= (x_i^*)^2 + \frac{t^2}{2} \end{aligned} \tag{3}$$

We model one acquisition which involves two firms. Suppose the two firms are firm 1 and firm 2 where firm 1 is the buyer or acquirer and firm 2 is the target or seller. The acquisition results in the shut-down of the target firm and all production shifts to firm 1. In this way, the total number of plants reduces from four to three. The resulting output of the acquirer post-acquisition is calculated as $x_{1,2}$ and the resulting profit as $\pi_{1,2}$. At equilibrium the following values are calculated:

$$\begin{aligned} x_{1,2}^* &= \frac{a + 10t - tZ_2 - 4tZ_1}{4} \\ \pi_{1,2}^* &= (x_{1,2}^*)^2 + \frac{t^2}{2} \end{aligned} \tag{4}$$

The acquisition takes place only if firm 1 can offer firm 2 at least π^*_2 and still be better off with its post-acquisition profit than remaining independent. So for a profitable acquisition to take place the following condition must hold

$$\Delta = \pi^*_{1,2} - \pi^*_1 - \pi^*_2 > 0 \tag{5}$$

Δ is defined as the profitability of the acquisition of firm 2 by firm 1.

2.3. Acquisition Decisions

The acquisition takes place as long as $\Delta > 0$. The profitability of acquisition and hence the likelihood that the deal takes place increases as Δ increases. The profitability of the acquisition can be expressed as a function of emission tax as follows:

$$\Delta(t) = \frac{-7a^2}{400} - \frac{at(14 + 4Z_1 - 11Z_2)}{40} + \frac{t^2(-36 + 8Z_1Z_2 - 16Z_1 + 44Z_2 - 15Z_2^2)}{16} \tag{6}$$

Even though the equation above suggests that Δ is quadratic in both t and a, we consider the special case where a is given as sufficiently high and t is the only parameter that affects the profitability of the acquisition of firm 2 by firm 1. Equation [6] shows that the acquisition decision (which depend on whether Δ is positive or not) relies on the level of emission tax. The emission tax affects Δ and the direction of relationship can go in different ways depending on the relationship between Z_1 and Z_2.

Before we examine some possible relationships between t and Δ, we note the following three points.

1. If firms 1 and 2 produce a 'clean' good with zero pollution intensity, both Z_1 and Z_2 would be zero. In this case, the proposed acquisition would not take place because $\Delta(t) = -[7a^2/400 + 7at/20 + 9t^2/4] < 0$.
2. If the acquisition partners are identical so that $Z_1 = Z_2 = Z$ the acquisition would still not be profitable because $\Delta(t) = -\frac{1}{400}[7a^2 + 70at(Z-2) + 25t^2(36 - 28Z + 7Z^2)] < 0$ for all $a, t, Z > 0$.

3. If $t = 0$, then the acquisition will not take place because it will not be profitable.

Equation [6] suggests that Δ is a quadratic function of t and it can be expressed as $\Delta(t) = \alpha t^2 + \beta t + \gamma$. The first and second derivatives of equation [6] with respect to emission tax can easily be calculated as $\Delta'(t) = 2\alpha t + \beta$ and $\Delta''(t) = 2\alpha$ respectively.

$$\alpha = \frac{-36 + 8Z_1Z_2 - 16Z_1 + 44Z_2 - 15Z_2^{\ 2}}{8}$$
$$\beta = \frac{-a(14 + 4Z_1 - 11Z_2)}{40} \tag{7}$$
$$\gamma = \frac{-7a^2}{400}$$

γ is the value of Δ when $t = 0$. The sign of β indicates the slope of $\Delta(t)$ when $t = 0$ and the sign of α determines whether this profitability function has a global minimum or a global maximum.

We know that $\gamma < 0$ always holds, but the signs of α and β depend on how Z_1 and Z_2 are related to each other and to the rest of the industry. We know that $Z_1 + Z_2 < H$ where we have assumed that $H = 10$. By setting $\Delta'(t) = 2\alpha t + \beta = 0$ we can find the value of t that optimizes the profitability of acquisition function. We denote this value as t^*. We assume that $\Delta(t) = \alpha t^2 + \beta t + \gamma$ has two real value solutions and we can solve for the two quadratic roots as $\hat{t}_1$ and $\hat{t}_2$ where $\hat{t}_2$ is the higher root. Using the quadratic formula we find that:

$$\hat{t}_2 = \frac{a[14 + 14Z_1 - 11Z_2 + 2\sqrt{2}\sqrt{2Z_2^2 + 2Z_1^2 - 4Z_1Z_2 - 7}]}{5[44Z_2 + 8Z_1Z_2 - 16Z_1 - 15Z_z^2 - 36]} \tag{8}$$

Table 1 represents all possible values for α and β and the implication for the acquisition decision. Case 1 and 2 suggest that the acquisition will take place as long as $t > \hat{t}_2$. In addition, t is directly related to Δ for all $\Delta > 0$. The sign of β does not really matter for the acquisition incentive in cases 1 and 2. Case 3 suggests that the acquisition occurs only within a certain range of emission tax ($\hat{t}_1 < t < \hat{t}_2$) and within this range there is an inverted U-shaped relationship between emission tax and profitability of the acquisition. Case 4 implies that no acquisition takes place. In the next section, we study some conditions that make α positive and discuss implications.

3. Special Case

Since we have not assumed anything regarding the pollution intensities of the acquirer and target, we will find what type of relationship between Z_1 and Z_2 make α positive. We use the software Mathematica by Wolfram to find conditions that make $\alpha > 0$ given that $Z_1 + Z_2 < 10$ and $a > 0$. We get the following output:

$$\frac{14(5-\sqrt{2})}{23} < Z_2 \frac{14(5+\sqrt{2})}{23} \quad \text{and} \quad \frac{15Z_2^2 + 36 - 44Z_2}{-16 + 8Z_2} < Z_1 < 10 - Z_2 \tag{9}$$

Table 1. Acquisition decision and the role of emission tax

Cases	α	β	t^*	Acquisition decision
1	$\alpha > 0$	$\beta > 0$	$t^* < 0$	$\Delta > 0$ for all $t > \hat{t}_2$
2	$\alpha > 0$	$\beta < 0$	$t^* > 0$	$\Delta > 0$ for all $t > \hat{t}_2$
3	$\alpha < 0$	$\beta > 0$	$t^* > 0$	$\Delta > 0$ for all $\hat{t}_1 < t < \hat{t}_2$
4	$\alpha < 0$	$\beta < 0$	$t^* < 0$	$\Delta < 0$ for all $t \geq 0$

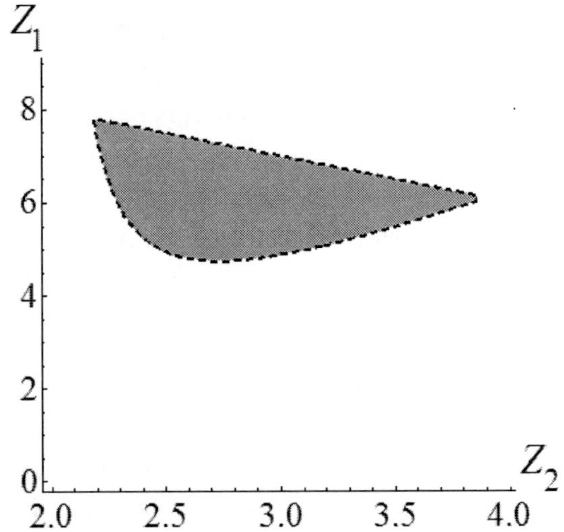

Figure 1. Relationship between Z_1 and Z_2.

Figure 1 presents these conditions graphically. The shaded region represents the relationship between Z_1 and Z_2 that make $\alpha > 0$. For all the cases represented in the shaded region $Z_1 > Z_2$. That is, the acquirer is 'dirtier' compared to the target firm. In other words the cleaner plant shuts down and post-acquisition production takes place using the dirtier plant. According to this result it is well possible that the acquirer seeks out a cleaner plant, but shuts it down without making use of its cleaner technology.

CONCLUSION

Even though most acquisitions take place among manufacturing firms regulated by environmental policies, there are not many studies which model acquisition decisions when such policies are present. In this book chapter, we model acquisition incentives when polluting firms compete in a Cournot oligopoly market. The findings of this chapter indicate that emission taxes, such as a carbon tax can affect acquisition incentives of regulated firms. Therefore, studies should incorporate pollution and environmental policy parameters into the model of acquisition decision.

The exact relationship between emission tax and acquisition (dis)incentives depends on the pollution intensity of the potential acquisition partners. We have found cases in which an increase in emission tax is directly related to the acquisition incentive. The findings of this chapter also suggest that there may be perverse incentive situations, namely cases in which dirtier firms profitably acquire cleaner firms without making use of their cleaner technology.

REFERENCES

Brookings. April 1, (2014). An EPA-Sanctioned State-Based Carbon Tax Could Reduce Emissions and Improve State Finances. Retrieved from http://www.brookings.edu/blogs/up-front/posts/2014/04/01-epa-carbon-tax-can-help-environment-state-finances-morris

Congressional Budget Office. May (2013). Effects of a Carbon Tax on the Economy and the Environment. Retrieved from http://www.cbo.gov/publication/44223

Fikru, M. G. (2014). Merger and Acquisition among Heterogeneous Polluting Firms: Theory and Evidence. Missouri University of Science and Technology Working Paper

Fikru, M. G. (2013). Environmental Policies, Mergers and Welfare. *Economia Mexicana CIDE*, *22*(2), 449-461

Fikru, M. G. & Lahiri, S. (2013). Can a Merger Take Place among Symmetric Firms? *Studies in Microeconomics*, *1*(2), 155-162

Fikru, M. G. & Insall, M. (2014). Modelling Potential acquisition decisions of polluting firms. Missouri University of Science and Technology.

Editors' Contact Information

Dr. Mahelet G. Fikru,
Department of Economics
Missouri University of Science and Technology
500 W 13th Street
Rolla, MO 65401 USA
Tel: (573) 341-6495
E-mail: fikruma@mst.edu

Dr. Matt Insall,
Department of Mathematics and Statistics
Missouri University of Science and Technology
315 Rolla Building
Rolla, MO 65409 USA
Tel: (573) 341-4901
E-mail: insall@mst.edu

INDEX

D

E

F

G

H

I

J

K

L

M

Q

R

S

T